THE
HUNT
for
FAITH
DISCARD

STEVE CHAPMAN

HARVEST HOUSE PUBLISHERS
EUGENE, OREGON

THE HUNT FOR FAITH
Copyright © 2018 by Steve Chapman
Published by Harvest House Publishers
Eugene, Oregon 97408
www.harvesthousepublishers.com

ISBN 978-0-7369-7424-0 (pbk.)
ISBN 978-0-7369-7425-7 (eBook)

Library of Congress Cataloging-in-Publication Data

Names: Chapman, Steve, author
Title: The hunt for faith / Steve Chapman.
Description: Eugene : Harvest House Publishers, 2018.
Identifiers: LCCN 2017061383 (print) | LCCN 2018015683 (ebook) | ISBN 9780736974257 (ebook) | ISBN 9780736974240 (pbk.)
Subjects: LCSH: Hunting—Religious aspects—Christianity. | Fishing—Religious aspects—Christianity.
Classification: LCC BV4597.4 (ebook) | LCC BV4597.4 .C335 2018 (print) | DDC 242/.68—dc23
LC record available at https://lccn.loc.gov/2017061383

Printed in the United States of America

18 19 20 21 22 23 24 25 26 / VP-GL / 10 9 8 7 6 5 4 3 2 1

To my fellow outdoorsmen and women...

My thanks to you for choosing to go with me via these pages into God's great outdoors, where so many life-changing lessons can be learned. It is my deepest honor to help guide you to some unforgettable trophies of truth that I hope will encourage you as you walk the trail of this life.

Steve Chapman

Contents

= 1 =

Always Hoping

...looking for the blessed hope and the appearing of the glory of our great God and Savior, Christ Jesus.

Titus 2:13

People who hunt and fish share a common attitude. As one who is happy doing either, I can testify that this shared mindset is nonstop while enthusiasts are in the woods or on the water. What is it? The answer is...we are always hoping.

Why does hope remain constant the entire time I'm out there doing what I love to do? It's because I'm in a place where I believe something exciting could happen at any moment. I'm *never* bored when I'm hunting or fishing because it's virtually impossible to be hopeful and bored at the same time.

I've also found that hope grows stronger when the time is nearing to head back to the truck or motor back to the dock. When I'm hunting, for example, and circumstances are about to bring an end to my adventure, such as a planned meeting that I can't miss or a setting sun, I get extra watchful and doubly hopeful. And if I haven't seen anything to that point, the intensity of the anticipation can reach lip-biting levels.

The same growing hopefulness also happens when I'm around water with a line and a rod. If I know I soon have to reel in, de-bait, and pull up anchor, my casting speeds up and the lure cuts the water just a little faster.

Why does this happen? Simply, I long for the hunt to yield an encounter with whatever I'm there to find. If I'm fishing, I deeply want to feel the tug on the line.

The hope that has kept me on the edge of my seat on a ladder stand or in a boat has served a good spiritual purpose. It has helped me as a follower of Christ to better understand the "blessed hope" of His appearing. Believing that it can happen any moment is indeed a sacred hope because it makes a life that is *never* boring and, more important, *never* hopeless.

One thing that makes the "blessed hope" grow even stronger in my heart is hearing the current and trusted teachers of Bible prophecy say with confidence that we're not far from Christ's return. To put it in hunter's terms, the moment is nearing to leave the woods, so it's time to listen harder and watch closer!

As one who is excited that the prophetic indicators point to a soon end of the age and the appearing of Christ as Redeemer of His people, my hope is intensifying. As it grows daily, I say with John the Revelator, "Amen. Even so, come, Lord Jesus" (Revelation 22:20 KJV).

> *God, I'm so grateful for the blessing of hope. I truly enjoy its benefit in the outdoors, but how much more wonderful is the hope that You will keep Your promise to return and deliver Your people from a world that is growing darker by the day. I want to be among those who are constantly excited, hoping and looking for Your appearance. By Your grace applied to my life, it will be so. Praise and glory be to Your mighty name. And...come quickly, Lord! Amen.*

2

Mounted Memories

Let this be a sign among you, so that when your children ask later, saying, "What do these stones mean to you?" then you shall say to them, "Because the waters of the Jordan were cut off before the ark of the covenant of the LORD; when it crossed the Jordan, the waters of the Jordan were cut off." So these stones shall become a memorial to the sons of Israel forever.

JOSHUA 4:6-7

If you are a hunter who has paid a pickup load of hard-earned money to a taxidermist to display one of your most prized trophies, surely you know that in the eyes of some folks, you're one shell short of a full clip. I'm not one of them.

If I enter your home (or your "cave" inside your home) where you have animals' parts on display, such as heads, antlers, tails, feet, or hides, I won't look puzzled or startled. Instead, I'll likely point to one of your cherished examples and say the words you hope most to hear: "Tell me about this one."

Before you can smile and respond to my request, I'll add some leading questions:

"Where and when did you get it?"

"What time of the day did the encounter happen?"

"Gun, bow, muzzleloader, pistol, or truck?"

"Distance of the shot?"

"Can you give me the name and phone number of the landowner where you got this one?" (I'll ask this question with a sheepish grin, but if you want to divulge the information, I won't refuse it.)

The reason I'll quiz you about the details behind the mount is simple—I like hearing a hunting story. My ear won't break if you're bending it with the details of your adventure. And it's even more enjoyable to see your eyes light up and your voice become excited as you look at your wall-mounted treasure and gladly cover the minute-by-minute, step-by-step, mile-by-mile account of your adventure. So bring it on. I'll give you all the time you want, and likely you'd do the same for me.

If you came to my house and asked me about the Alaska brown bear cape, the fan and double beard from a huge Tennessee gobbler, the Michigan buck, the South Dakota mule deer, my son's first deer, or the Arizona javelina, you'd see my face glow as I offered the details of their stories.

When a hunter sees a fellow hunter's walled evidence of success and asks to hear the story about it, the pricey mount has accomplished its intended purpose. We understand and appreciate this reason for displaying our trophies, and that's why we can easily understand the purpose of the large stones the Israelites placed in the Jordan River as they entered the Promised Land (Joshua 4). The stones were placed there to memorialize a very significant event—God's deliverance of the people of Israel from their enemies and the safe passage of the ark of the covenant to the other side of the Jordan on dry ground.

When the men who placed the testimonial stones in the river were later asked by their children to tell the story behind them, perhaps the fathers replied the way hunters do when asked about one of their mounted memories. No doubt there was joy in their eyes as well as praise on their lips for the One who had miraculously delivered His people.

Perhaps you have a story about your own "Jordan River" experience and God's gracious intervention. If so, may He bless your willingness to let others know about it, and may your testimony of His goodness be an encouragement to anyone who says, "Tell me about this one."

God, some events in my past are marked with the remembrance of Your timely and helpful intervention. Thank You for those experiences. When I have the opportunity to tell others, especially children, about Your deliverance, I will do it with great joy and in hope that the story will give You the praise You deserve. In Your mighty name I pray. Amen.

3

Smell like a Barn

I have become all things to all people so that by all
possible means I might save some. I do all this for the
sake of the gospel, that I may share in its blessings.

1 Corinthians 9:22-23 niv

I'm not a tobacco user, but I am a hunter who has used tobacco smoke.

Through the years, the Tennessee county I live in has claimed the number one position in US tobacco growth and production. Planting begins around midspring, and harvesting starts sometime in August. Most of the harvested tobacco is hung in barns along rural roads. In some of these barns, the plants are simply drying. But many of the structures are built for "dark firing" the leaf-laden stalks with smoke from a well-controlled, slow-burning pile of hardwoods.

One of the barns is near our house and is owned by a farmer who lets me hunt on his property. I walked by it one day in late August when it was active and took in the aroma of the smoke that was boiling out into the air. As I did, I suddenly got an idea. When I returned home, I made a phone call to ask the farmer a question.

"Mr. Walker, would you object to my bringing my camo clothes

to your tobacco barn around the third week in September and letting them 'marinate' in the smoke for a few days?"

Before he could ask why I would want to do such an odd thing,
I said, "Archery deer season starts at the end of September, and since
the local herd is used to the smell of the smoke coming from the
barns around here, I'm thinking I could probably outsmart their
noses if I smelled like a barn when I'm in the stand."

Mr. Walker commended me for my scent cover idea and agreed
to let me try it out using his barn. When the time came to "dark
fire" my clothes, I put two pairs of pants, a couple of shirts and
undershirts, a face mask, socks, and gloves on metal hangers and
hung them along the inside wall. Almost a week later, I gathered my
smoke-infused gear, put it in a plastic trash bag, and stored it in the
covered bed of my pickup. The smoky aroma couldn't be contained
in the bag and filled the cab, but I didn't mind.

On the third morning of bow season, I was in a ladder stand next
to a field. I knew the weather conditions were pushing my scent
to the ground, but I wasn't too concerned because I smelled like a
tobacco barn from head to toe. About twenty minutes after sunrise,
my scent cover tactic paid off when a sizable buck walked under me,
stopped and put his nose in the air, and showed no concern what-
soever. I'm convinced that as mature and well trained as his olfac-
tory system was, the only reason he didn't run when he checked the
wind was that he thought he got a whiff of a local smoking barn.

I really like recalling the memory of that hunt for two reasons.
First, there's nothing like getting a fresh hunting idea, trying it, and
seeing it work. Second, I always enjoy discovering a connection
between a hunting experience and God's written Word, and in this
case I realized that to some extent my "smell like a barn" method
resembled the biblical approach to evangelism that the apostle Paul
used:

To the Jews I became like a Jew, to win the Jews. To those under the law I became like one under the law (though I myself am not under the law), so as to win those under the law…to the weak I became weak, to win the weak. I have become all things to all people so that by all possible means I might save some (1 Corinthians 9:20,22 NIV).

Becoming "all things to all people" is an evangelistic method that can be as effective now as it was in Paul's time. I have a feeling that if Paul were here today and wanted to win those who hunt, he would find a way to appeal to them even though he had never been a hunter. Perhaps he would wear camo while he preached or volunteer to be the camp cook for a group of guys on an elk hunt. By doing so, he would "smell" familiar to the hunters he was with, and they would be far more likely to be open to his message.

The difference between my reason for smelling like a tobacco barn and Paul's reason for becoming all things to all people was that my intention was to deceive the deer while Paul's purpose was to help his listeners find the eternal truths of Christ and His saving grace. And just as I didn't become a deer to win a deer, Paul didn't become a sinner to win a sinner. He was careful to remain faithful to Christ as he shared the gospel with those who needed to hear it. May God help us do the same.

Dear Lord, thank You for every opportunity to share the gospel with others. I pray for wisdom to know how I can present the message of Your love in an appealing manner. And I ask for Your guidance and grace never to stray from You while I'm among the lost. In Christ's name I pray. Amen.

— 4 —

A Little Beyond

He went a little beyond them, and fell to the ground
and began to pray that if it were possible, the hour
might pass Him by. And He was saying, "Abba!
Father! All things are possible for You; remove this cup
from Me; yet not what I will, but what You will."

Mark 14:35-36

When my buddy Lindsey and I are hunting spring gobblers, one of us will often say to the other, "Go up ahead and check over that rise to see if there's anything in the field." It's a tactic we enlisted after realizing that when we walked together, we sometimes produced too much noise or movement to avoid detection by turkeys.

One particular field, which we have visited annually, definitely requires checking initially with only one set of eyes. On the west and southwest portions, the hillside rises abruptly to the fence that stands between the woods and the grassy openness, leaving little room to hide once we get to where we can peek into the field.

The northwest and east entrances are very flat and wide open. We can hide behind some sizable trees at the field edge when we approach on our hands and knees, but it's just too risky for both of us to make the crawl at the same time.

Our goal is to avoid getting busted by the wary birds that live there, so you can understand why we have to resort to just one of us stealthily going ahead to get a visual of the field. The one who stays back watches the other like a hawk, looking for a quiet wave to come on, or in some happy instances, seeing him excitedly give that universal signal that turkey hunters love to see—a raised arm and curled fist shake that says, "Gobbler spotted—game on!"

We usually take turns being the one to go ahead. Each of us trusts the other to do it carefully and effectively enough not to mess up and send the boy and girl birds flying to the next farm. And I must admit that it's pure fun (for the human). The intense feeling of anticipation while engaging in the quiet stalking maneuver is one of the things that keeps turkey hunters going back to the fields and woods.

When the duty falls on me to go forward and check things out, I don't even try to hide the wide-eyed joy on my face as I gather my gear and happily march—that is, crawl—away. I am, for lack of a better word, giddy about going. It's an elation that lingers long after the hunt, and I thoroughly enjoy recalling it even at this moment. As I do, my thoughts turn to the opening words of Mark 14:35. Speaking of Jesus, the verse begins, "He went a little beyond them."

That day in the Garden of Gethsemane, knowing that He was nearing the time when He would be crucified, Jesus went ahead of the disciples with a heavy heart. There was no feeling of joy, though there was a sense of anticipation—the terrifying kind. He was surely aware of the Romans' skill when it came to torture. They were masters at inflicting pain and putting humans to death. No wonder He fell to His knees and entreated the Father in heaven to let the cup of woe pass by Him. Yet as we all know, He faced the cruel cross and gave His life for our redemption.

Someday on a future hunt, if you're with a friend and one of you says to the other, "Go up ahead and check things out," perhaps you'll remember what took place not long after it was said of Jesus, "He went a little beyond them." May it bring a feeling of gratitude to your heart as it does mine for what He willingly did for the sake of our redemption.

Jesus, I offer You my deepest thanks for giving Your life on the cross for my salvation. When You went ahead of the disciples to pray, perhaps they didn't know what great anguish You felt. They know now, and so do we, and we praise You for enduring it. May all the glory be Yours and Yours alone forever. Amen.

Scars in the Yard

May you live to enjoy your grandchildren.
Psalm 128:6 nlt

For many hunters, any excuse to get outside in the summer is welcome. Of course, fishing could easily top the list of off-hunting-season things to do, but I'm quite satisfied with outdoor activities that are closer to home—like mowing. As far as I'm concerned, mowing the yard is a perfectly good substitute for being inside. Besides, my weekly walks behind our push mower lead me to a place on our property where I'm always reminded to pray for some very special people in my life.

Thanks to my green-thumbed wife, our backyard is a lovely place. However, I see four bare spots each time I mow. They're like dirt scars on a beautiful grass body, and normally I would heal them with some seed and hay. However, I've come to love the yard scars and dread the day when they're not there. Here's why.

Three of the six-feet-long, oval-shaped marks were made over time by the feet of our six visiting grandkids as they played on the swings hanging from the Amish-built set behind our garage. The fourth scar is circular and about three feet in diameter. It was made by our grandson George on the day he discovered that a garden hose, a spade, and dirt are the three main ingredients for making mud.

When I'm mowing and I come to the four scars, I get a little melancholy because I know that when the grass has filled in those spots, the grandkids will probably have outgrown their excitement about going to DeDe and Papa's house. That's when the swings will be empty and motionless, and the little voices that reverberated in the backyard will be silent. No more sweet sounds of "Push me, Papa!" or "Get the hose and the little shovel for me, Papa."

When the quiet returns to the yard behind our house, I hope I'm not foolish enough to resent the absence of our grandkids. To do so might steal the joy in the memories of their visits, the echo of the noise they made while running and playing, and the remembrance of the smiles that were often framed with chocolate ice cream or watermelon juice.

Most of all, if time goes on and I'm still around when the grandchildren aren't, I want to be grateful that I actually lived long enough to enjoy them. My time with them has been a blessing that I'll always treasure. Until then, my plan is to maintain the prayer-prompting scars in the yard. That's what a garden hoe and water hose are for!

Thank You, Lord, that my days have carried me into grandparenthood. I pray that while my grandkids are young, You will protect them and help me be Your light to them as they grow. And someday, when their visits are few and far between, I pray that Your hand will continue to guide them on their journey through time. And thank You so much for the scars in the yard that remind me to lift them to You. Amen.

The One You Got

*He who sits on the throne said, "Behold, I
am making all things new."*
Revelation 21:5

I arrived at the farm for an evening hunt, lowered the tailgate of
my truck, and opened my well-worn bow case. As I lifted out
the compound, I noticed that some of the setscrews showed little
spots of rust, the string was looking a bit frayed, the rubber coating
on my two-prong rest was worn, and the silver metal underneath
was beginning to peek through. I noted it was time for some main-
tenance on the bow, but I figured it had one more hunt in it before
that chore.

A little while after climbing into my stand, I rested the bow
on my lap and gave it another visual check over. As I did, I started
thinking about how much easier it would be simply to replace the
aging arrow flinger. Since there was no movement in the woods, I
took out my phone and began browsing some online sites to get an
idea of prices for a new compound.

"Whoa!" I hadn't bought a new bow in a long time. I couldn't
believe the cost of the latest models. The words "government loan"

came to mind. It was not a good time economically to be tempting myself with photos and reviews of what was available in the archery world. I knew I had just one option. I didn't want to do what had to be done, but it always helps to say the obvious aloud: "Work with the one you got!"

A week later I picked up my repaired bow from a local archery shop, and the tech assured me it was in good working order. In fact, he said he was actually very pleased to get to work on what he considered a vintage compound. I left there feeling very good about my decision, and my wallet was smiling too.

I thought again of that choice to keep the aging bow as I sat with several hundred men from surrounding churches, listening to a keynote speaker. He was encouraging us to be better members at our local congregations, especially when it came to supporting those in leadership. Recognizing the fact that congregations will always have individuals who are not happy with their pastor, he paused strategically as he looked at the roomful of men, and then he offered an unforgettable challenge.

"Fellows, some of you here tonight wish you had a new pastor. Well, if you want a new pastor, pray for the one you got!" His statement had a familiar ring to it, and immediately I had a mental image of my refurbished compound. At the same moment, several guys in the room simultaneously said, "Amen!" I wondered how many of them were pastors who were grateful for the speaker's support.

On the way home from the event, I thought about how good it would be if all of us who were gathered at the church decided to apply the speaker's challenge not only to our current pastors but to other relationships in life. Before I got to our driveway, the following song was nearly completed.

Pray for the One You Got

If you want a new pastor, pray for the one you got
If you want a new neighbor, pray for the one you got

If you want a new husband, pray for the one you got
And, brother, if you want a new wife, why not pray for
   the one you got

Pray, pray, pray for the one you got
No need to trade the old one in
God can make things new again
Pray, pray, pray for the one you got

If you want a new boss man, pray for the one you got
If you want a new nation, pray for the one you got
If you want a new mother-in-law, pray for the one you
   got
Sister, if you want a new body, why not pray for the
   one you got

And what about yourself
Are you tired of who you are?
If you want a brand-new you
Here's where you start

Pray, pray, pray for the one you got
No need to trade the old one in
God can make things new again
Pray, pray, pray for the one you got![1]

Lord, thank You that You are fully able to take that which is old and make it brand-new. Instead of discarding or discounting the value of those who are in my life, I know it's best to bring them to You and allow You to change them where needed. And I admit that I can always be improved. Help me to be a willing patient in Your hands as You restore me. May it be done for Your glory and Yours alone! In the name of Jesus, amen.

7

You Can Reel 'Em In

No one can come to Me unless the Father who sent Me
draws him; and I will raise him up on the last day.
JOHN 6:44

I had the unforgettable privilege of helping George, my four-year-old grandson, dig his first tub of fishing worms, put them on a hook, and catch his first fish. What a day it was.

George's eyes bugged at the sight of the wiggly bait we found when we turned over rocks, stepping-stones, and old logs in our yard. As I knelt to look in the dark, moist places where worms hide, he leaned over my back with his chin pressed on my shoulder next to my ear. He couldn't contain his excitement when he spotted a wiggler. When he did, my aging, sensitive eardrums rattled with the sound of his young voice yelling, "There's one, Papa! Now we can go fishing!"

"We need a few more worms, George. Let's keep looking." Without complaining about delaying our departure to where the fish lived, he followed me around the yard and helped me find more bait. The search went on for about twenty minutes—a long time for a kid to wait.

Finally, we buckled up in the truck and headed to a friend's twenty-acre lake about fifteen miles from our home. George practically jumped out of his car seat after I parked bankside at a spot where it looked both bluegill-ish and safe for a rambunctious boy. All I had for him to use was a man-sized rod and reel—not ideal equipment for a youngster, but he didn't know.

Within a couple of minutes, I had a bobber on the line and an Eagle hook baited with a juicy worm. Asking George to join me at the water's edge, I considered letting him try the first cast, but I knew there were inherent dangers for both of us that could be avoided. I really didn't want to call his folks and break the news that one of us, especially their son, was on the way to the ER to get a barbed hook removed from a cheek—or worse, an eye. So I pushed the button on the closed-face reel and tossed the line about ten yards into the lake.

I knelt down, pulled George in next to me, and said, "Now, watch that bobber floating in the water. If you see it bouncing, a fish is eating the worm. If the bobber goes all the way under, we need to pull quickly and set the hook so we can catch 'im!"

Of course, George didn't know what I meant by "set the hook," but I figured it's never too early to let him hear some fishin' talk.

I repeated "Watch the bobber" a couple of times, and he must have detected the excitement I was feeling. The breathy sound of his voice as he said, "Okay, Papa," told me he felt the anticipation too. That was exactly what I was hoping for.

Within half a minute, the bobber suddenly hopped up and down—but stayed afloat. I felt George jump as he yelled, "It bounced, Papa!"

"Yes, but let's wait till it goes under, and when it does, I'll catch him and you can reel him in."

We waited quietly for about ten seconds. Then it happened—the bobber dove out of sight. I quickly raised the rod tip. I could feel the fish was caught when the line went tight and the rod bent forward. Wanting George to feel what it was like to have a fish on the hook, I helped him tighten his hold on the rod and said, "Feel it, George? Do you feel the pull?"

The fish wasn't huge, but it gave enough fight to introduce my Grand-Chap to the thrill of the tug.

"I can feel it, Papa!" Those were sweet words to hear.

Confident that it was a bluegill that was not going to get away, I showed George how to crank the handle on the reel and bring the fish toward us. He gave the handle a few turns and then did what seems to be an instinct for little boys—he stopped reeling and started backing up. It was working for him, and I didn't tell him to do any different.

When the bluegill slid up onto the grassy bank, I helped George reel up the slack in the line so he could lift his catch off the ground. The fish flipped wildly and swung toward him. I thought he'd drop the rod and run, but he didn't. Instead, he held on and said something in kid language that I didn't quite understand—but it sounded like "Help!"

I grabbed the line with my left hand, held the fish in my right hand, and invited George to feel how slick the scales were. He cautiously slid his finger over the slimy side of the fish and said, "Eww!" I showed him the fins and explained how they helped the fish swim, and I lifted one of its gills to show how it breathed. It was more than he would remember, but again, it's never too early.

I got some pictures on my phone of George and his first fish. After quickly texting one of them to his parents and his Grandmother Chapman, we let the fish go back to "his mom," as George put it. Then we caught a few more bluegill along with a nice bass that gave the new angler a very memorable fight (which I got on video—thank the Lord for phones with that capability). Then we headed back to our house with an intermediate stop at a fast-food window. That day was a great memory for sure.

A couple of days later as I recalled the outing with George, I thought about how I was the one who actually caught the fish, but I let my grandson enjoy the thrill of reeling it in. We were a team, and both of us were fully satisfied with the outcome, to say the least. Then it occurred to me that what George and I experienced is a great picture of what happens when a follower of Christ leads a nonbeliever to a relationship with Him.

On the surface, it may appear that a believer who does the preaching or witnessing is the one who catches the fish, but the truth is, God is the One who hooks them through the miraculous work of His Holy Spirit. In the end, though, just as George and I went home happy, both God and the fisherman are joyful for the catch.

May we who seek to bring the hope of Christ to those who swim in the waters of hopelessness always, and humbly, remember that though we are "fishers of men," God is the One who does the catching. He just lets us reel 'em in.

Thank You, Father, for the great privilege of being a fisher of men for You. I know that You alone can draw a lost one to Yourself. I don't have the power to do it, but You have granted me the honor of offering the blessed bait of the gospel to those who need to hear it. Lead me to the lost, and use me, O Lord, to present Your hope to them. For Your glory and for their salvation, may it be so. In Christ's name I pray. Amen.

8

A Thorny Situation

Thorns and snares are in the way of the perverse;
He who guards himself will be far from them.

PROVERBS 22:5

Everything about rabbit hunting is total fun except for one unwelcome thing—thorns. I love the sound of a beagle's bawl when his nose picks up the scent of a cottontail. I enjoy the feel of my finger on my gun safety as I intensely watch and wait for the rabbit to circle in front of the dogs and come back within range. I cherish the companionship of my shotgun-toting comrades and the conversation we exchange in the field over a thermos of hot coffee. And of course, there's the taste of tender rabbit stew to love. But I can do without the thorns.

If I had kept and mended all the overalls and the camo-colored pants and shirts that have been ripped to shreds by the merciless clawed bushes I've pressed through, I think I could outfit an army battalion. And if I had all the blood that has seeped from the wounds inflicted by thorns on my tender skin, I could stock the Red Cross blood bank with plenty of O positive.

As annoying and painful as thorns can be, here's a cold, hard fact I have to face: I've never had a single thorn come and find me. Whenever I've winced at the sting of a sharp, pointed barb as it tore at my skin or heard the cash-consuming rip of a spike rending my clothing, it was due to a solitary reason: I put myself in the situation.

Of course, the key to not feeling the hurtful effects of thorns is to avoid them. I realize that some encounters with thorns are unintentional, such as having to retrieve a rabbit that came to its final resting place inside a clump of briars, or having to crash through some thornbushes to quickly get to a spot where a circling rabbit might reappear.

A run-in with pain-inflicting briars can happen while chasing rabbits, but I'm always looking for a way to avoid it. If I have to walk or run several extra yards to get around a patch of briars, I'll make the effort. I'd be crazy not to. In the same way that I do what I can to avoid feeling the vicious grab of thorn branches, I want to do what's necessary to avoid the spiritual thorns and snares in this world.

Proverbs 22:5 mentions one thorn that can wound a man's spirit. The first part of the verse warns, "Thorns and snares are in the way of the perverse." Being perverse means using for evil something that God created as good. The Bible warns against perversity in our…

Speech. "Let no unwholesome word proceed from your mouth, but only such a word as is good for edification according to the need of the moment, so that it will give grace to those who hear" (Ephesians 4:29).

Justice. We are warned not to take or offer bribes (Proverbs 17:23), oppress the poor (Amos 5:12), kill the innocent (Exodus 23:7), and bear false witness (Proverbs 19:5).

Sexuality. First Corinthians 6:9-10 lists some specific sexual perversions, including homosexuality, adultery, and fornication.

The second part of Proverbs 22:5 offers some skin-saving advice for anyone who wants to avoid the thorns of perversion: "He who guards himself will be far from them." That means that the first step to bypassing the pain that spiritual thorns can cause is not to entertain or engage in perverseness. It sounds simple to do, but because the human heart is prone to sin, it's not always so easy.

Thankfully, God has given us a way to recognize perversity and keep a safe distance from it. It's being willing to pray humbly and sincerely the prayer that King David offered to God: "See if there be any wicked way in me, and lead me in the way everlasting" (Psalm 139:24 kjv).

Father God, thank You for loving me enough to see if there is any wicked way in me and for leading me around those destructive barbs of sin. You know very well that I sometimes put myself in situations where thorns and snares cause me pain. Thank You for forgiving me when I do. Help me remain faithfully determined to stay as far away as I can from the thorns of sin and perversity. Oh, how I need Your grace! I ask for it now in the name of Jesus. Amen.

9

Things Change Prayers

…with all prayer and supplication in the Spirit,
and watching thereunto with all perseverance.

Ephesians 6:18 kjv

The well-known adage "Prayer changes things" is undeniably true. But did you ever consider that *things change prayers*? For example, let's say a huge elk is standing broadside three hundred yards from you, and it has an impressive seven-by-seven rack—potentially one for the record books. A gusty wind is pounding your face and making your eyes water, and worse, it starts to sleet, and your scope lens begins to fog.

The massive bull takes a few steps forward and stops, but he's now behind a pair of trees, and the only thing showing is his vitals between the trunks. You put the crosshairs on his shoulder and push the safety off. As you take a deep breath and hold it, you whisper a prayer—but what prayer will it be?

If you want to make the deadly shot because of what's rising majestically above the bull's skull, and the bragging rights that go with it, then your prayer would be worded one way. However, if times have gotten hard for you, and now the winter survival of your family depends on you making a life-sustaining, meat-yielding shot, then you would surely pray another way. In other words, a thing called hunger has changed your prayer.

Of course, hunger is not the only prayer changer. Horror can do it too, as in the case of a bear hunter whose excited morning prayer at the base of the mountain is, "Lord, bless me as I head up to hunt the mighty bear." An hour later, on a high ridge where the hunter inadvertently surprises and seriously upsets a huge grizzly, he might desperately pray, "God, have mercy on me and deliver me from this angry beast!"

James 5:13-15 shows at least three other things that can change our prayers.

> Is anyone among you *suffering*? Then he must pray. Is anyone *cheerful*? He is to sing praises. Is anyone among you *sick*? Then he must call for the elders of the church and they are to pray over him, anointing him with oil in the name of the Lord; and the prayer offered in faith will restore the one who is sick, and the Lord will raise him up, and if he has committed sins, they will be forgiven him (emphasis mine).

The individuals in the verses weren't always hurting, happy, or unhealthy, but something happened to change their situation, and as a result, it changed their prayers. This can happen to any of us in these categories or any other, and it can happen at any time. We do well always to remember not only that prayer changes things, but also that we must be ready to go a different direction when things change prayers.

Devote yourselves to prayer, keeping alert
in it with an attitude of thanksgiving.

COLOSSIANS 4:2

God, I want always to be willing and ready to change the way I pray. I know that at times I'll have little or no warning about a situation that requires flexibility in praying. I need Your grace and mercy to be ready for these surprises. What a great comfort to know You're never caught off guard by them. Thank You for hearing my prayers, whatever the need. Amen.

· 10 ·

Hello for Me

*Jesus said to her, "I am the resurrection and
the life; he who believes in Me will live even
if he dies, and everyone who lives and believes
in Me will never die. Do you believe this?"*
JOHN 11:25-26

I received a letter from a mother that contained heart-wrenching news about the unexpected death of her young son. His absence, she said, was especially noticed whenever the family had dinner together. The empty chair and missing place setting were constant reminders of the loss they all felt.

The most poignant words in the letter were in reference to their mealtime prayer. Whoever said grace would always end with, "Amen…and, Lord, please tell Jimmy hello for us."

The mother said that even though she didn't know whether God approved of or honored this prayer, making the request was somehow comforting. I appreciated her admission of uncertainty about the prayer, but I also understood why the family would offer it. I have said the same thing to God, except I was asking Him to say hello to my late father.

I don't know if my hellos are divinely forwarded, but like the mother of the absent son, I am somehow consoled to think that maybe, just maybe, God says to my dad, "Your son says hello!" After all, according to John 11:25-26, if anyone believes in Jesus, even though he dies he will live and never die. By faith I believe my dad is alive in heaven, so I prefer to think Jesus could easily relay a message to him for me.

The mother's letter about her absent son inspired me to write the following song lyrics. Maybe the words will bring solace to you if someone you love is "on the other side" and you wish they could get a hello from you. Who knows—maybe they can!

Tell My Boy Hello for Me

Unmade bed, clothes on the floor
Earnhardt poster hanging on the door
Not a single thing has changed
Since the day that phone call came

His mother stands in his quiet room
Thinking, *How could he leave so soon?*
Tears fall down, she lifts her head
Looks up to heaven and says

"Tell my boy hello for me
God, I'm asking, would You please
Tell him just how much he's missed
Let him know how much I wish
He was here right now, back with our family
God, would You please tell my boy hello for me?"

November day, up on the hill
Golden sunrise, the wind is still
Perfect day to wait for deer
But there's been a change this year

His father can't believe it's true
He's alone in the stand he built for two

But he's sure his son wants him there
He points to heaven and says a prayer

"Tell my boy hello for me
God, I'm asking, would You please
Tell him just how much he's missed
Let him know how much I wish
He was here right now, sitting next to me
God, would You please tell my boy hello for me?"[2]

Thank You, God, that Your people don't have to grieve as do those who have no hope. I trust that those I love who died as believers in Jesus are living with You now. How I long to see them again, and because of You, I will. But until then, if You are willing, let them know of my love for them. In the living and loving name of Jesus, amen.

11

In the Record Book

The city has no need of the sun or of the moon to shine on it, for the glory of God has illumined it, and its lamp is the Lamb...and nothing unclean, and no one who practices abomination and lying, shall ever come into it, but only those whose names are written in the Lamb's book of life.

REVELATION 21:23,27

When I speak at wild-game dinner events, I get to enjoy hearing stories from attendees about their exploits in the woods. In some cases, deer hunters who have bagged big-antlered trophies don't provide a point count. Instead, they describe the racks using the "total inches" method.

For example, they might say, "Yeah, I'm guessing he was every bit a 143 buck," or "I had him scored, and the final tally was a 176."

If nonhunters hear a three-digit reference to a deer's antlers, they'll likely respond with a tilt of the head and blank stare, otherwise known as the "dog look." However, avid deer hunters will probably respond, "Dude, that's awesome!"

Why? Because they know that the numbers reflect the total of the measurements of various lengths, including main beams, tines, points, and spread.

When someone uses total inches to describe a deer they've tagged, it tells me that one of the reasons they hunt may be to see their name on one of the prestigious pages of the record books. For that reason, their hunting season can be a long stretch of days filled with thinking, dreaming, and scheming about how they can be there when the "big one" comes into range.

Of course, there's nothing wrong with wanting to bag a big buck for the books. In fact, being disciplined enough to do so can help a hunter develop important inner strengths, such as patience and confidence, not to mention the physical benefit of endurance. And the quest even brings a spiritual advantage. It can be a very good reminder that there's another book in which every hunter should want their name to be recorded. It's called the Lamb's book of life, and it's mentioned in Revelation 21:23-27.

Unlike the hunting record books that contain the names of those who have taken an animal from life to death, the names written in the heavenly record book are of those whom God has brought from death to life through Christ. They are, so to speak, God's trophies of grace. And because of Him, they are guaranteed eternal residence in the new Jerusalem, where there will be no need of the sun or moon for light because the glory of God will illuminate it. What an awesome, peaceful place to look forward to.

With such a generous promise to all who will accept it, who wouldn't want their name written down in the Lamb's book of life? I certainly do, and by God's boundless mercy and grace, I can trust that it is. How about your name—is it in the heavenly record book?

Nevertheless do not rejoice in this, that the
spirits are subject to you, but rejoice that
your names are recorded in heaven.

LUKE 10:20

*Father in heaven, as one of Your followers, I am immensely
and profoundly grateful that You have written my name in
Your Lamb's book of life. I admit that to have my name in
that book is infinitely more important than seeing my name
in a book of records here on the earth. Forgive me for getting
so distracted by temporal pursuits that I would forget the eternal goal of being found on the pages that name those who are
Your own. In the blessed name of Christ I pray. Amen.*

12

Dye Bomb

Behold, you have sinned against the LORD,
and be sure your sin will find you out.

NUMBERS 32:23

I won't forget the video I saw online that showed a hunter sneaking through a patch of woods when suddenly there was an explosion at his feet. He had unknowingly caught a trip wire with his boot and pulled the trigger on a dye bomb. The contents instantly covered him head to toe, and he choked and gagged as he ripped off his eyeglasses, which were dripping with the material. Watching him try to wipe the spray off was comical as he discovered that the more he tried, the worse it spread.

The incident was shot on a trail camera but shown in black and white, so I couldn't tell if the spray was white, yellow, red, or some other intensely bright color, but one thing I could see was that the man was going to have to wear it home.

Apparently, the guy who owned the property was having trouble with the uninvited hunter and decided to catch him in the act of trespassing. Drenching him with a surprise blast of identifying dye was punishment enough, but filming it and then broadcasting it online for the world to see was the icing on the embarrassment cake. His "sin" had definitely found him out, and since he didn't have a change of clothes or a change of skin to hide the evidence of his transgression, others were sure to know about it too.

I replayed the clip a few times, and a couple of interesting questions came to mind in regard to the eventual unmasking of a secret sin.

- Does all sin find us out publicly as it did for the dye-doused man caught on the trail cam?
- Is it always necessary for a sin to be revealed publicly for the sake of correction?

From personal experience I can say the answer to both questions is, not necessarily. I candidly confess that I've had less-than-stellar sin moments that no human would have known about unless I had revealed them. I can cite one example from many years ago that involves hunting.

I was set up at the edge of a field when the landowner suddenly drove his truck into it. I hadn't yet received his permission to be there. Right behind me was a dry creek bed, and in one fluid motion I grabbed my gear, rolled backward into the ditch, and stayed out of sight as he drove toward me. He stopped briefly at the exact spot I had been just seconds earlier, and then he drove on.

I was utterly relieved that I avoided a confrontation with the landowner, but I was not happy. Deep feelings of regret for my deceitful decision found me out. I may not have been wearing a blast of gunk from a dye bomb for others to see as evidence of my failure, but I privately saw it, and like an ugly stain on my heart, I secretly wore the dye of guilt for years. The only thing that was effective in removing it was repentance. Thank God for His grace and forgiveness.

Sadly, the farmer died before I found the nerve to confess that

I had disrespected him and his property in such a deceitful way. Though I trust that by God's grace I have been forgiven for my wrongdoing, I admit that I still occasionally wrestle with the shame of it. The fight reminds me that the pleasure of sin, especially the hidden kind, is just not worth the pain it causes in the soul. Live and learn.

> *Thank You, Father, for allowing sin to find us out even when others don't see it. Sometimes that outcome hurts even more than public repentance. Thank You that Your cleansing forgiveness reaches even those sins. I pray in the words of Your holy Son Jesus that You would lead me not into temptation but deliver me from evil so that my soul won't be covered with the stain of sin and guilt. To Your glory I ask this in Christ's holy name. Amen.*

13

Battle with the Buzz

Catch the foxes for us,
The little foxes that are ruining the vineyards,
While our vineyards are in blossom.
SONG OF SOLOMON 2:15

Though most of us have heard the ancient saying "It's the little foxes that spoil the vine," it bears repeating. This bit of biblical wisdom has the potential to spare all of us from eventual destruction if we heed its warning. Elwood McQuaid, author and chief editor of *Israel My Glory*, the Friends of Israel magazine, offers some valuable insight about the quip in his excellent book *Not to the Strong*.

> In our lives we are seldom confronted by imperial-size problems. When we are, most of us are well prepared as to the proper course of action to pursue. The immensity of great crisis situations dwarfs our ability to respond adequately. We therefore quickly prostrate ourselves before God to seek out His solution. But really, most of our problems are more like terrier-size…confrontations. It is with such problems that we frequently experience failure.

The late Dr. James McGinlay told the story of an experience he had while preaching in the Canadian wilderness. One snowy afternoon he decided to engage a sleigh for a jaunt in the woods. At a particularly picturesque spot in the road, he stopped the sleigh and ventured forth on foot. Suddenly, while walking around a large tree, he found himself face-to-face with an enormous bear. Needless to say, he beat a hasty and somewhat unceremonious retreat.

Dr. McGinlay contrasted this experience with another encounter he had at a summer conference in Florida. A short time after retiring one night, he heard the incessant whine of a flying mosquito piercing the silence. He popped out of bed to do battle with his tiny tormentor. But when the light went on, the adversary was nowhere to be found. Throughout the night, the grim little disquieter eluded Dr. McGinlay's most determined efforts to destroy his foe. The next morning the revered lecturer went on his way, frayed and testy.

He concluded that there was sort of a dignity born of crisis in the bear-sized problem. But it was the mosquito that inflicted the most devastating wounds.

How true! And what a familiar ring that tale has for us. This is where we live. It is the great battleground of life. It is here that we rise or fall as overcomers—in the day-to-day, while the rounds of repetitious responsibilities grind away at us. We keep waiting for something big to happen to us. It seldom does. But then, after all, why should Satan use cannons, when small darts can more effectively accomplish his purposes?

We conclude that our prayerlessness, neglect of personal communion with God, unwieldy tempers, proneness to procrastinate, and the like most often cause us to become the bedfellows of defeat. Our attention must be fixed on being victorious in these areas, if we ever expect to be prepared to face the larger issues of the Christian life.[3]

My thanks to Elwood McQuaid and the staff of Friends of Israel for this memorable and helpful look at the destructive potential of the "little sins" in life that too often go unchecked. Perhaps this ever-timely warning will come to mind the next time you're hunting and see a fox, or you're battling with the buzz of a mosquito around your head, or you suddenly disturb a giant bear! If it's the latter, it would be a good idea to mull over the wisdom while you're running.

Father in heaven, thank You for the help You give in those times when the major trials attack me, but I also want to give You thanks for helping me boldly deal with the everyday sins that can just as easily, and sometimes more effectively, ruin my life. Blessed be Your name for being my deliverer. Amen.

14

A Book in the Text

So they made Him a supper there.
JOHN 12:2

Only someone like my wife, who knows how much work goes into getting ready for a dinner guest, especially one of great importance, would know how much effort is implied in John 12:2. Annie will tell you that "So they made Him a supper there" may be a statement just seven words long, but it could easily have represented seven hours of work. In cell phone vernacular, it may have been a text-size sentence, but there is a book in the text.

Hunters also understand what "a book in the text" means. Suppose a friend from an East Coast town is hunting in one of the big western states, and he sends his buddy a text that says, "Went out this morning; took a bull." The amount of time and effort summed up by those few words would not be lost on his hunting friend back east.

I've taken a few trips out west in pursuit of elk. On just the day the shot is taken, there is so much to do. It starts with waking up extremely early, preparing and taking in some necessary nourishment, gathering gear, walking or riding a horse or a four-wheeler in the dark for an hour or two, glassing the mountains, maybe stalking, probably climbing, setting up for the shot, finding the downed animal, tagging it, field dressing it, enduring the backbreaking haul of the meat back to camp, and preparing supper (if there's energy left). After that, there's at least one more thing to do before collapsing in a sleeping bag. If a cell signal is available, the bone-tired hunter sends a text to loved ones at home to report about the day, using the few words his tired mind can put together.

Even a brief text—"Safe back at spike camp…having a great time"—would say a lot more than meets the eye. Dreaming about the trip for months or years, finally committing to it by buying the license with hard-earned cash, making list after list of what to take and what gear to buy, driving to the firing range several times to make sure the weapon is sighted in, counting out the pushups and miles run to get in shape—these are just a few of the numerous things the short message could imply.

Yes, the endless details involved in a hunt can be summed up in just a short sentence. Many other effort-packed events in life can also be reported in text-size statements. Think about these:

- We're going on vacation.
- Our daughter just had a baby!
- We're moving to a new house.
- We finally sold our house.
- I graduated from college.
- My brother learned to fly.
- My wife made dinner!

Thinking about how much work is involved in these few everyday examples boggles the mind. But as complex and extensive as the effort is in each one, the amount of work represented by all of them combined can't compare to what is included in the grandest of all "texts": "In the beginning God created the heavens and the earth."

Thankfully, the verses that follow Genesis 1:1 elaborate on the amazing work of God's hands, but the descriptions of each of the six days of His work are limited overviews of the innumerable things He did to create the universe. The fact that so much information about God must be said in so few words makes Him seem even bigger, more fascinating, and more worthy of endless praise. I for one can't wait to see and hear what's not mentioned in those biblical text-size sentences.

Father in heaven, You know our fleshly minds cannot contain the full report of all You've done or will do. If all Your mighty acts were recorded in detail, the world itself would not contain the books that would be written. For that reason I'm grateful for Your plan to give me a new body so that when I enter eternity I will be able to take it all in. Until then I will take note of Your greatness found in Your divine "text." Amen.

15

Sinkhole

The prudent see danger and take refuge,
but the simple keep going and pay the penalty.
PROVERBS 22:3 NIV

After hunting in middle Tennessee for many years, I was made aware of an inherent health risk I had not considered. The heads-up came one afternoon when I stopped to say hello to the owner of the farm I was going to hunt. Knowing that I frequented a particular twenty-acre, deer-friendly section of his property, he asked, "Are you going to the big patch of woods on the other side of the power lines?"

I answered, "That's my plan."

"Well, I just wanted to let you know I found a sinkhole there a couple of days ago, and it's already pretty deep."

I was sure he could hear the worry in my voice when I asked exactly where it was.

"It's just to the right of where you enter the woods on the logging road. If you go to the stand you put up, you'll pass by the hole on your way in. And if you come out after dark, please be careful."

I thanked him for the warning, and before I drove away he offered a little bit of history about sinkhole activity in the area, including the story of the "big one" that appeared on his farm long before I met him. He said he was plowing when suddenly the ground beneath him gave way. The next thing he knew, the earth seemed to be swallowing both him and his tractor.

Though the incident had occurred years earlier, the panic he felt at the moment seemed to return as he told the story, especially the part about having to use his partially upright tractor as a ladder to climb out of the hole. He was happy to report that his only injuries were a few bruises, and best of all, a contractor managed to rescue his tractor later that day using a huge crane.

Feeling even more cautious after hearing of the farmer's close call with being buried alive, I thanked him again for the warning and proceeded to the field gate where I usually parked. I thought about abandoning my plan to go to the logging road stand to avoid the sinkhole, but I had never seen one up close and couldn't resist checking it out.

Finding the round depression in the ground wasn't hard. When I got within about ten yards of it, I stopped to gawk at the nearly twenty-foot-wide, perfectly circular hole. Then, driven by curiosity to take a peek down in it, I stepped forward all the way to the very edge of the hole. It appeared to be at least half as deep as it was wide.

As I stood there staring down into the unusual sight, a couple of questions suddenly came to me that gave me chills. *Just how fragile is the earth around this hole? And is my 180 pounds enough to cause it to get bigger and deeper?*

The mental image of me being swallowed by a hungry sinkhole instantly made my knees weak. Without hesitating an extra second, I began to slowly and lightly step backward as if I were doing a reverse sneak. When I was far enough away from the edge to feel safe again, I turned and headed down the logging road to my stand.

The rest of the afternoon and evening, I watched for deer that never showed up. All the while I felt very thankful that I avoided a fate similar to that of the people mentioned in Numbers 16:32: "The earth opened its mouth and swallowed them up"!

As for my exit from the woods after the sun went down, I took an alternate route back to my truck just to be sure that the farm didn't get a chance to eat me.

I didn't take a deer home with me that evening, but I did come away from that hunt with an unforgettable memory. I'll always remember how anxious I instantly felt when it dawned on me how dangerous it was to be standing on the ledge of the developing hole. As much as I would have liked to linger and study such an intriguing sight, denying myself that pleasure was definitely the right thing to do. I can still recall how utterly relieved I felt when I backed away from the mouth of the hole far enough to stop my knees from shaking.

The sinkhole encounter is actually more than just an extraordinary memory in my mental scrapbook. It's a very good reminder of what to do when I suddenly sense spiritual danger. The smart decision in that moment is not to ignore the inner warning but to back away from the threat and go to the safe and solid ground to which prudence can lead me. If I choose to continue entertaining the hazard, I can end up paying the penalty of being swallowed, so to speak, by a spiritual sinkhole. That's a disastrous fall I'd rather not experience.

God, You know well that I'm journeying through a world full of deep and dangerous spiritual pits that I need to avoid. I pray You will help me recognize them and resist the temptation to keep walking toward them. I ask for Your help to make this wise choice not only for my good but for the purpose of bringing glory to Your name. Amen.

16

Scattered

He who is a hired hand, and not a shepherd,
who is not the owner of the sheep, sees the wolf
coming, and leaves the sheep and flees, and
the wolf snatches them and scatters them.
JOHN 10:12

My first spring turkey season was incredibly enjoyable (for me, not for the turkey). I was so "spurred" by the challenge that I averaged three days of hunting each week during the six-week season. As the closing date neared, I told my friend who had introduced me to the challenge how much I dreaded not being allowed to hunt birds again until a year had passed. He listened graciously and then broke some good news to me.

"Hey, man, being a newbie, you're apparently not aware that we have a fall turkey season in our state."

I almost did a jig when I heard I had to wait only six months to hunt the big birds again—that is, until he continued talking.

"Of course, hunting turkeys in the fall is not like spring hunting. In the spring we use our hen calls, and the toms give away their location by gobbling back at us. But in the fall we have to hunt 'em sort of like we do deer—we have to be there when they walk through."

He could tell I was a little worried about what he had just told me and was quick to add, "But there's a way we can hunt turkeys in the latter part of the year that can be just as enjoyable as the spring hunt. We find a bunch, bust 'em up, and then call 'em back in."

Seeing I had no idea what he was talking about, he gave me an explanation. "If I encounter a flock of birds in the fall, I know there's no way to defeat all those well-trained eyes. I don't attempt to hide and wait. Instead, I just take off running at 'em and make 'em scatter. Once they're all out of sight, I find a place to sit where I'm least likely to be seen, and I start calling with a series of short, high-pitched whistles with my mouth. It's known as a 'kee-kee,' or gathering call. In a few minutes, they'll start regrouping toward the kee-kee sound. Now I only have to hide from one pair of eyes at a time, and if I do it right, I'll fill a fall turkey tag."

It was good to know I wouldn't have to wait a full twelve months to go "turkey takin'." Around August, when the hunting juices were really starting to flow, I thought about the scattering tactic again. As I imagined trying it, I remembered that the Scriptures mentioned something about scattering. I did a word search, and sure enough, I found what I was looking for in John 10, verse 12.

The verse is in the passage about a man who owned some sheep and employed a temporary shepherd. Because the hired hand didn't own the sheep and didn't care for them as much as their owner did, it was a no-brainer for him to run away when a hungry wolf invaded and scattered the flock. By isolating the individual sheep, the predator had an easier time overcoming its prey.

The wolf is not the only one who knows this method works—and thus the point of the story. God has a flock made up of believers, and the wolf from hell, the devil himself, is always ready to capture one at a time by scattering them from the others. His final goal is the consumption of us all.

How can this happen? The devourer of our souls can come running into the Lord's flock through technology, partial truths, errant doctrine, jealousy, greed, deadly habits, entertainment, hatred, unforgiveness, and even misguided tolerance, to name a few ways. When we scatter and are left alone with our vices and devices, our minds become fertile hunting grounds for the wolf.

Now, when fall rolls around and I begin to think about chasing turkeys, I can't help but be reminded of the "bust 'em up" ploy that my mentor taught me. I also remember once again that when it comes to being a member of God's flock, I want to stay on guard spiritually by keeping close to the Shepherd who cares for me and who can keep me from falling victim to the devil's scattering trick.

Oh loving Shepherd, I'm grateful that Your care for me never fades, especially when the wolf of this world comes near and tries to isolate me. Help me never to be drawn away from the safety of the fold by his trickery. I pray this for my flock-mates too, that we would not be caught and scattered. May it be so in the name of our great and caring Shepherd, Christ Jesus. Amen.

17

Sun Brand

*It came about when Moses was coming down from
Mount Sinai (and the two tablets of the testimony
were in Moses' hand as he was coming down from the
mountain), that Moses did not know that the skin of
his face shone because of his speaking with [the Lord].*

EXODUS 34:29

After unhooking the line from the dock cleat, I stepped into
my friend's big, fancy, high-powered fishing boat and settled
into the passenger seat. As I applied sunblock to my nose and cheeks,
he started the monstrous motor and then pushed the throttle lever
slightly forward. The engine rumbled at a low level as we slowly
moved away from the dock. "We have to go about a quarter of a
mile to get beyond the no-wake zone," he said. "After that, I won't
waste any time getting to my favorite bass spot."

I didn't realize that he was giving me a warning. I failed to
respond appropriately, but he was patient with me and waited until
we were within a few yards of open water before he explained what
he meant.

"Uh...you might want to turn your cap around before I throttle up." The mischievous smile on his face told me that something wild was about to happen. I was right!

When the boat crossed the border of the no-wake zone, he pushed the throttle all the way forward. The engine roared, and I felt my body press hard against the seat back. In just a few seconds, the calm breeze crossing the bow increased to hurricane force against my face.

Ah, so *that's* why I needed to turn my cap around. If I hadn't, the wind would have caught it under the bill and immediately blown it into the lake. So for the rest of the day, through several more eye-watering rides to other fishing holes, I left my cap in the reverse position. It wasn't until the afternoon when we were at the dock again that I turned it back around.

When I got home and walked in the house, I removed my cap. Annie met me in the kitchen, and when she said hello, her eyes went to my forehead. She didn't stop looking at it as she said, "That's gotta hurt."

I had no idea what she was referring to. "What do you mean?"

She grimaced as she said with a tone of pity, "You might want to go look in the mirror."

Wondering what she meant, I went to our hallway bathroom and looked at myself in the mirror. I was shocked at what I saw. It looked as though someone had taken a fiery hot, half-moon-shaped brand and stamped my forehead with it between my eyebrows and my receded hairline. The obvious half-circle burn was not going to go away anytime soon.

"You know we're scheduled to appear on a TV show tomorrow in Kansas City." Then she attempted to console me. "I have makeup that might cover that sunspot." Thankfully, but with more layers applied than I preferred, she managed to make me look mostly normal on camera.

That odd-shaped, bright-red sun brand on my face comes to

mind when I read in Exodus about Moses coming down from Mount Sinai with his countenance aglow. Of course, the skin on his face was radiating for a much different reason than mine did. It was because he had been speaking with God face-to-face.

Is it possible to spend enough time in the presence of the Son that the evidence is visible to others? The answer is yes! Our skin won't glow like Moses's did, but there are other signs that can prove we have walked and talked with God. Here are a few:

- *Joy.* "You will make known to me the path of life; in Your presence is fullness of joy" (Psalm 16:11).

- *Love.* "No one has seen God at any time; if we love one another, God abides in us, and His love is perfected in us" (1 John 4:12).

- *Rest.* "My presence shall go with you, and I will give you rest" (Exodus 33:14).

The truth is, we can't spend time with God without being "branded" by His influence in our lives. We may not even know that His character, or glory, is showing—but others will. And the best result will be that He will get the glory.

Father in heaven, I bless You for the privilege of walking with You on this trail of time. As I do, I pray that You will help me stay close to You and often speak with You so that my life will become a display of Your grace and mercy. And as the light of Your goodness shines through me, may others see that You are real and be drawn to You. May I decrease so that You will increase. I ask in the name of Jesus that this would be so to Your glory alone. Amen.

·18·

Vines and Branches

I am the vine, you are the branches; he who
abides in Me and I in him, he bears much
fruit, for apart from Me you can do nothing.
JOHN 15:5

Early August has traditionally been the time when I head to the woods before deer season to check my elevated stands for needed repairs or upgrades. I have often arrived at a familiar tree and discovered that since the previous season, some unwanted floral decoration has adorned the stand ladder or climbing steps—vines!

Whether it's Virginia creeper, poison ivy, grape, or any other clinging crawlers, they are not welcome because they hinder my access to the stand platform. The effort required to eliminate them varies with their type. Some of the tender vines, such as honeysuckle, can be easily pulled away from the tree. Others aren't so simple to remove due to the thickness of their main trunk and how tightly they hug the tree.

To eliminate the hardier types, I use a three-step process. First, with my handheld pruning shears I cut the main trunk of each vine at the base of the tree. Next, I wait about two weeks to let the vine and its tangling branches above the cut die and dry out.

When I return to complete the process, I've found that the job requires a lot less effort because of how easily the lifeless, withered vines let go of the tree. Speaking from experience, it would have taken twice the energy and triple the sweat to remove them prior to cutting off their life source—not to mention the anger I would have had to control.

The process of de-vining my stands is a good illustration of the vine imagery found in John 15:5. Jesus says of Himself, "I am the vine," and of His followers He says, "you are the branches." Then He goes on to say (my paraphrase), "As long as you're attached to me, you'll have life and bear fruit. But if you don't, you'll die, and you won't be able to do anything." It's an outcome I certainly don't want—but the devil does.

If Satan had his way, not only would there be no branches, but there would be no vine to have branches. He tried to sever Christ from mankind at the cross, but thankfully the resurrection foiled his evil scheme. Since he failed with that attempt, Satan now wants to cut the branches off the vine. But we have good reason to believe that will never happen, because Jesus said, "He who abides in Me and I in him, he bears much fruit."

For me to abide in Christ and Him in me is not a mystical thing. Instead, it's a very real activity that involves being grafted into Him by His grace through repentance, feeding on His written Word, letting it fill my mind, and allowing it to direct my will and convert my desires to match His affections.

In addition, abiding in Christ means that I may have to submit to God's pruning knife from time to time and let Him cut away unwanted tendrils of idolatry, jealousy, laziness, or any other sinful tendency that would keep me from wholeheartedly remaining in Him. Though it might not be enjoyable, I'll take His love-motivated, life-sustaining pruning any day over the deadly cutting that the devil wants to do.

Father in heaven, what kindness You have shown by making me one of Your branches. I pray for Your will to be done in my life. If You see a worthless way in me, cut it off. Continue to nourish me with Your marvelous Word and help me abide in You now and forever. I ask that this be done to Your glory. In Christ's name, amen.

19

Do What He Said

So Samuel did what the LORD said.
1 SAMUEL 16:4

Anyone who has hunted with a skilled guide knows the value of listening to wise instructions. I was reminded of this during an elk hunt in Montana.

On the fourth day of a five-day hunt, we were walking out of a wooded area, nearing a wide-open field that was quite steep. Just before we reached the last few trees, the guide stopped abruptly, dropped to both knees, and motioned for me to stop and hunker down. He put his binoculars to his eyes and glassed the mountainside. When he lowered his binoculars to his chest and turned to me, I could tell by his expression that the news was good.

Using his knees as feet, he backed up and got beside me. He whispered, "I want you to crawl up to that short, dome-shaped rock near the edge of the woods and get a good rest with your rifle. As you crawl ahead of me, you'll see the bull feeding at about 250 yards. I'll come right behind you and help keep an eye on him too." I did what he said.

In the distance, I saw the bull the guide had seen, and suddenly

I had to fight to crawl without shaking. After reaching the rock, I set my backpack on it and used it to steadily cradle my rifle. When I was confident about my setup, I found the bull in my scope. My heart was pounding like a kick drum in a dance tune.

"Steve, the wind is heavy, blowing right to left at probably twenty-five miles an hour. Aim a few inches above his back. I don't think the bull is nervous, so let him get still and broadside."

Less than a minute later, the six-by-six leisurely turned perfectly broadside in my scope with his head on the left side of the sight picture. I pushed the safety button to the off position, gently pulled on the trigger, and let the rifle surprise me when it fired. I quickly found the bull in my scope again, and he acted as if nothing had happened. In fact, it hadn't.

Sounding like a very experienced sergeant, the guide looked through his binoculars and asked, "Did you put the crosshairs straight above his heart area?"

I whispered, "I did."

Calmly the guide added, "I think the wind got that bullet 'cause it didn't connect. Fortunately he didn't even flinch. The wind is so strong and noisy, the shot was probably just a dull thump in his ears. He's still not nervous. This time, aim four or five inches above his back with the crosshairs on the very back portion of his lungs. Let the wind do the rest of the work." I did what he said.

When my rifle settled back into its rest after the second shot, I couldn't find the bull in my scope. The guide said, "He's very hurt and headed up the mountain."

We waited a few minutes, gathered our gear, and quickly climbed the steep terrain. My guide led me well inside the woods to lessen the possibility of being spotted by the other elk on the mountainside. My lungs were burning when we reached a flat about three hundred yards uphill. We arrived about the same time the bull did. I had only a few seconds before the bull escaped into some very heavy timber, so my guide said, "You'll need to shoot using your knee as a rest." It was not my favorite option, but I did what he said.

I dropped to the classic one-knee shooting position and looked for the injured bull in my scope. He was struggling as he walked slowly toward the dense timber. He was about seventy-five yards away and unaware of our presence. When he stopped momentarily, the blast of my gun roared across the mountainside. The third shot closed the deal.

Several times during that hunt with my elk guide, I had opportunities to do what he said, and the memory of the hunt has helped me through the years to remember an important spiritual truth. If I expect to be victorious as a God-follower in this life, my best option is to listen to my heavenly Guide. When He gives me instructions, I always need to be like Samuel, who "did what the LORD said."

God, how grateful I am that You love me enough to want to guide me through the sometimes treacherous and challenging terrain of time. Thank You for providing Your written Word that contains Your instructions for me to follow. I want to do what You say, and I ask for Your grace and strength to follow through. To Your glory, may it be so. In Christ's name, amen.

20

Measuring Line

*I lifted up my eyes and looked, and behold, there
was a man with a measuring line in his hand.*

ZECHARIAH 2:1

When I read the opening sentence of Zechariah 2, the imagery of a man with a measuring line reminds me of something I observed when I was the guest speaker at a wild-game dinner.

I arrived early for a sound check and finished the process with time to spare before the meal was served. I took the opportunity to browse the tables lining the walls of the building and saw plenty of hunting gear and handmade crafts. Many of the attendees were checking out the wares, but the biggest crowd was gathered around a table where a man was measuring antlers.

At the close of the event, one of the grand prizes was to be awarded to the set of antlers that garnered the highest score. There were quite a few entries, and the gentleman who was measuring the racks was working as fast as he could.

As he stretched his measuring line across the tines, I could see in the not-so-excited demeanor of some of the hunters that they didn't expect to win the top prize. They knew the antlers they entered were only a little above average, so I assumed they were just curious to get a total number. There were others, however, whose bucks sported larger racks, and the expressions on their faces seemed to indicate that they thought they had a shot at taking home the grand prize.

I enjoyed watching the measuring process and overhearing bits and pieces of the stories behind the antlers. I was impressed with how many friendly smiles and sincere congrats were being offered with the tales of hunts. It was an entertaining time of eavesdropping. That's when I thought about two brothers who, if they had been in the line, might not have been as brotherly with each other as the guys at the church were. Likely, their fiercely competitive spirit would not be as pleasant to behold.

From the time the brothers had been very young, each one approached deer season with the goal of outdoing the other. When they were on the stand, they weren't relaxing, reflecting, and learning valuable lessons about life from the insight-rich challenge of outsmarting the wary whitetail. Rather, they were consumed with one goal—to win the battle for the biggest buck. Their egos were on the line. Their mood throughout each season was dark, and the one who ended up with the smaller rack would try to make up for the deficit by killing more does.

As sad as it was to see the brothers engage in such a hollow competition, it helped me see the kind of hunter I don't want to be. I'd rather measure success in other ways than tine length or tip spread. Their ugly rivalry reminded me that there are much better ways to measure success—by taking an extra doe to share with a needy family. Or by spending memorable time with a son, a daughter, or a friend. Or by taking a kid hunting for the first time so he or she can experience the incredible thrill of being up close and personal with a deer.

As for the two brothers who ruined many seasons with self-centered hunting, they could have benefited from a visit from the man with the measuring line mentioned in Zechariah 2. Who was he? Many Bible scholars agree that He was the Angel of the Lord, the Messiah Himself, who appeared for the purpose of measuring the boundaries of the city of Jerusalem in advance of its restoration. I'm sure He could help the two brothers—and anyone else who measures success in fruitless ways—to restore a good attitude about hunting.

Father in heaven, I want You to be my measurer of success. Show me anything in me that comes short of Your will for my life. Measure my heart, and wherever restoration is needed, please do the work that You alone can do. In the immeasurably wonderful name of Jesus I pray. Amen.

21

In a Little While

A little while, and the wicked will be no more;
though you look for them, they will not be found.
But the meek will inherit the land
and enjoy peace and prosperity.
Psalm 37:10-11 niv

When I was a younger hunter, I often sat in the woods for hours without a single worrisome thought. All that was on my mind was which critter might appear in the next moment and the thrilling challenge of outsmarting its eyes or its nose or both. But that was before having a wife, raising children, and then having in-laws and grandchildren in the picture. All these loved ones deserve my attention and the best care I can give them, so for many years now, when I've been in the quiet of a deer stand, my thoughts have not always focused on the hunt.

Lately, one concern for these precious people in my life has been for their safety in a world where violence seems to be rampant. It's as though the forces of hell have been unleashed on our nation. Especially troublesome are the groups that are forming with the sole purpose of terrorizing and killing innocent people.

I confess that at times when I'm in the stillness of the woods, I imagine the grim possibilities of having to defend my family against those whose mission is evil. Sometimes I have gripped my gun or bow a little tighter as I considered what I would do if any of my loved ones fell victim to the deviant actions of a terrorist.

I know there is only one way to effectively combat such disturbing images so that I don't weary myself with them. It is the same thing David did when he was distressed. First Samuel 30:6 reads, "David strengthened himself in the LORD his God." Following his lead, I know I have to deliberately and consciously give the Lord my dread and trust that He will oversee the safety of my family. I've found that when I rest in that hope, I sense a growing confidence that God will overcome any wickedness that my family or I might face.

The good news is, the craziness and madness in our world will not go on forever (though sometimes it seems as if it will). Psalm 37:10 promises, "A little while, and the wicked will be no more" (NIV). In other words, God is going to see to it that the evil violence and all who promote it will come to an end.

But wait! The psalm offers even more assurance in verses 12 through 15.

> The wicked plots against the righteous
> And gnashes at him with his teeth.
> The Lord laughs at him,
> For He sees his day is coming.
> The wicked have drawn the sword and bent their bow
> To cast down the afflicted and the needy,
> To slay those who are upright in conduct.
> Their sword will enter their own heart,
> And their bows will be broken.

I take great courage from the fact that these verses don't include any tentative language at all. They never refer to what God *might* do. All I see is what He *will* do. The wicked *will* be no more, and their bows *will* be broken.

I've found that when the daily news is all bad, it's good to reread Psalm 37 because it lifts my spirit again and bolsters my trust in God, who, without question, will have the final say about the wicked. In fact, you can not only read about it—you can sing about it too. If you're so inclined, feel free to make up your own melody to this lyrical summary of Psalm 37.

In Just a Little While

The wicked bend their bow
And they draw their sword
To bring down the righteous
The needy, and the poor

But God is a Warrior
He'll come against our foes
Their sword will cut their own hearts
And He will break their bow

So don't you worry
Don't you be afraid
God is gonna win in the end
He's gonna have His say
Lift up your head
Let heaven see you smile
'Cause the wicked will be no more
In just a little while

Like flowers in a field
Where a fire glows
The enemies of God
Will go up in smoke
While the meek and the blameless
Are safe in His care

When evil comes against us
Our God will be there

So don't you worry
Don't you be afraid
God is gonna win in the end
He's gonna have His say
Lift up your head
Let heaven see you smile
'Cause the wicked will be no more
In just a little while[4]

All-powerful God, I take great comfort in knowing that just as You made the sun to rise and bring an end to the darkness of night, in a little while Your risen Son will bring an end to the spiritual darkness in this world. Your soon coming and sure triumph over every form of wickedness brings such deep hope to my soul as I think of my loved ones. Thank You even now for the peace that we will enjoy because of Your care for us. Blessed be Your mighty name forever. Amen.

22

Available

Now there were six stone water jars there for the Jewish rites of purification, each holding twenty or thirty gallons. Jesus said to the servants, "Fill the jars with water."

JOHN 2:6-7 ESV

Sitting for hours on a deer stand provides time for reading and meditating on God's written Word. It's especially enjoyable and always beneficial to look at familiar Bible stories in search of a helpful, yet-to-be-discovered insight tucked away in the details.

As an example, consider John's account of the wedding at Cana where Jesus performed His first miracle. Six unused stone water jars played an important role in the story. What happened to them can provide encouragement to anyone who may feel overlooked or unuseful. To explain what I mean, I've taken some liberty to humanize the jars and imagine what one of them might say if asked to speak for the entire group.

Available

I was among the empty ones standing in the hall
We assumed there'd be no use for us that day at all

Didn't know that we were special, just vessels made of
  stone
Not chosen for the wedding, set aside and left alone

Now we could hear the sound of cheer for the bride
  and the groom
Then a woman said, "Son, their wine is gone, it's
  happened much too soon"
To those who serve, she said these words: "Do what He
  says to do!"
Then He looked our way and pointed, the next thing
  that we knew...

He said, "Fill them up with water, fill them to the
  brim!"
And as they did something changed deep within
They say we held a miracle, the taste of heaven's vine
But we were just available to be used by the One
Who turned the water into wine

I hope someday someone will take the time to write it
  down
'Cause what happened here could calm the fear of
  those who have their doubt
That they have worth while here on earth, may they
  not forget
What Jesus did with jars of stone He can do with
  hearts of flesh[5]

I realize I'm probably risking my reputation by saying I was encouraged by a talking stone jar—but it's true. It really is inspiring to think that Jesus can and will use whoever is available regardless of their place in life.

As for me, I want to stand by and be ready for the moment when He points at me and says, "Fill him up with water!" When He gives the order and I submit to it as a useful vessel, I can be confident that whatever He uses me for will be a blessing to others.

God, how grateful I am that You would choose to use me for Your work. I want to serve You in any way You desire. Do fill this vessel of flesh with the water of Your Spirit, and I will give You the glory for any good that comes of it. In the name of Your miracle-working Son I pray, amen.

23

Drawn In

*No one can come to Me unless the Father who sent Me
draws him; and I will raise him up on the last day.*

JOHN 6:44

I was never sure what the breed mixture was in Mark the Dog, but he seemed to have some Labrador retriever somewhere in his history. I met him when he was a scrawny, abandoned puppy, and it was in the most unlikely place.

On a cold winter Sunday morning, after taking more time than we had to get our two kids ready for church, warm up the car, and deice the windshield, we were a little late for Sunday school. Abandoning our usual routine of walking in together, I dropped off Annie and our eight- and five-year-old children at the front entrance and hurried around the building to find a place to park.

No one else was in the lot as I exited the car and headed to the back door of the church. When I was a few feet away from it, some movement caught my eye to my left. In a shadowy, bricked cove, I saw a small bundle of golden-brown fur. It was a tiny dog, crouching and shivering. When our eyes met, the helpless little creature looked at me with an expression that seemed to ask, "Where's my mommy?"

I stepped back toward the parking lot and looked around for several seconds for an adult parent dog in the area, but it was quiet and empty except for the two dozen or so cars parked there. I went back to the puppy, and as if I had no control to do otherwise, I gingerly picked it up and cradled his frail body.

Finding no collar or any other sign of ownership, I made a snap decision. I was sure our kids were in their classroom and Annie was in our adult class. I hurried to our car, put the dog in the front seat, and headed home. During the ten-minute drive, I turned the temperature knob to high to help him warm up.

At the house, I went to the garage and got a cardboard box for our new and maybe temporary guest. After putting a bowl of water and a biscuit in the box, I carefully lowered the tender stray into its rescue home and went back to church.

When I sat down next to Annie in the classroom, she whispered, "Where have you been?"

I smiled and said, "I'll tell you later."

When our family got home from church, I took everyone to the basement. The furry puppy was sitting quietly in the box. The kids gasped with joy when they saw him. Annie gasped too, but it wasn't with joy.

"What is this?" she asked. But her tone hinted, "Ain't no way."

"Uh…it's a dog, babe. And it's a boy." My smile was bigger than both our kids' smiles put together, and Annie knew we had just acquired our first family pet.

I explained where I found the puppy, how its facial expression broke my heart, and how I couldn't resist rescuing the little guy. Annie said, "Well, we need to name him. We're studying the book of Mark in Sunday school, so let's name him Mark…the Dog."

We all agreed on his name and took turns hugging, petting, feeding, and cleaning up after Mark until the sad day he left us.

Our dog resembled the breeds that love retrieving birds, but he didn't have a hunting bone in his body. Mark was a city dog. Still, he was well-loved. He not only provided great memories for me and my family to enjoy, but also taught me a valuable lesson that I treasure in my heart.

John 6 says that our heavenly Father draws us to Himself, and Romans 2:4 says that the kindness of God leads us to repentance. I can understand these verses better when I think of how I drew Mark to myself that day at the church. My kindness toward him and his great need for me led him to accept me. That sounds like how God wooed me to Himself.

During the time Mark was with us, I got to know him better and better each day. Our kids loved the dog, and even Annie was won over by him. We made him a part of our family. That sounds like what God did for each of us.

This analogy has its limits in that Mark, a canine, could never become one with us humans. But our relationship with God goes way beyond that. First Corinthians 6:17 says, "Whoever is united with the Lord is one with him in spirit" (NIV). What an amazing and life-changing thought that the God of the universe would actually draw us in and then make us more than a houseguest. He joins us to Himself.

We have a picture of our kids with Mark the Dog. It hangs on the wall on my side of the bed, and it's often the first thing I see in the morning and the last sight I see at night. How grateful I am for that photo reminder of the fact that I was drawn in by the almighty and ever-loving God.

Father in heaven, there are not enough words to say thank You for the love You showed to me by inviting me in to Yourself. Like Mark the Dog, I was spiritually cold and abandoned by the world. Yet You drew me in and took me home. Your kindness continues to lead me to repentance, and Your mercy is new every morning. Blessed be Your name. Amen.

24

Where the Fish Go

Peace I leave with you; My peace I give to you;
not as the world gives do I give to you. Do not let
your heart be troubled, nor let it be fearful.
JOHN 14:27

When our son and daughter were young, our family had an eighteen-foot fish and ski boat that we enjoyed. When I wasn't out on the lake wetting a line for crappie, bass, and (whether I wanted them or not) catfish, I was piloting our water rocket with kids behind it tubing and skiing. The summer fun and fish dinners the boat provided were marvelous.

Our kids especially enjoyed having me churn up the water and create waves so they could get "big air" on their tubes. The higher they flew above the water, the greater the thrill. Each face was one gigantic smile as they hung on to their tubes for dear life during a long, sweeping turn. The speed that the maneuver created was just frightening enough to be fun, and when the fat, round, circle of inflated rubber slid up onto the four-foot waves, the launch brought screams of joy that still echo in my head. Most of time the kids couldn't hold on, but getting dumped was part of the fun.

The area that we favored for the wet and wild tube rides was one of the sections of the lake that seemed to host a lot of fish. We never knew if there'd be a boat or two already at that spot with anglers in them glaring at us when we approached. The sight of a sparkly fiberglass motorboat filled with kids and colorful tubes always spelled trouble to those sitting serenely on their perch seats with rod and reel in their hands. Because I liked fishing too and knew how bothersome tubers can be, I made sure to find another part of the lake that was not occupied.

Not long ago our pastor said something during a sermon that made me think of a summer day years earlier when the kids and I were fortunate to be the only boaters at our favored spot. Referring to the peace Christ can give mentioned in John 14:27, he said, "The kind of peace that is spoken of in this verse is deep and constant, like the calm that a fish experiences below the surface of the water while a major storm above him is creating massive white-capped waves. The world can't offer calm like that. It's found only in going deep in your faith in the Lord."

When I heard our pastor's analogy, I was suddenly in our family boat way back when we had it. In my memory we were at the place on the lake we favored and the fish favored too. I remembered looking behind me at the waves I had created and thinking, *I bet the fish hate all the commotion.*

It wasn't until I heard our pastor's description of the kind of peace that God gives that I realized those fish at the lake were not bothered in the least by our frequent chaos-creating visits. When the world above them turned dangerously tumultuous, they did what smart fish do—they just went deeper. They went to the place where their hearts were not troubled, neither were they afraid.

I left church that Sunday with more than an enjoyable memory of a day on the lake with our kids. I left with a new lease on peace as well. Just as the fish go deep to find calm, I want to go deep in the waters of faith. It's the one place I can find the peace that the world can't give.

> *Lord and giver of peace, thank You for a place to go when the sea of this life is churning. While dreadful storms of fear, doubt, sickness, sorrow, and wars are creating emotional and spiritual havoc, I want to be found swimming in the deep assurance of Your presence. That's the greatest possible place of rest. I praise You for the depth of Your love for me. In Christ's name, amen.*

25

Wind in the Cornfield

For momentary, light affliction is producing for us an
eternal weight of glory far beyond all comparison.
2 CORINTHIANS 4:17

My dictionary says the word "affliction" refers to "a state of pain, distress, or grief; misery." Just reading the terms associated with the word makes me shiver, and it makes me wonder how anything of value could come from affliction. Yet the Word of God assures me there is good to be gleaned from it.

I don't go out looking for affliction of any kind, but I know that from time to time it will find me, and when it does, I must allow it to work for me instead of against me. Thankfully, an experience while bowhunting in the vastness of a Midwestern state helped me see how trouble can produce triumph.

I was the guest of a North Dakota hunter, and it was the last afternoon of a three-day attempt to fill a mule deer buck tag. I spent the first day sitting on a stool between two large round hay bales, hoping to ambush a passing mulie as he headed to or from a feeding area.

Nothing.

The second day was spent walking the hills, spotting, and hoping to find a buck that would stand still long enough for me to sneak in for a close, sure shot.

Nada.

The third day was a bust in the morning, and during lunch my host decided to call a friend of his who had several hundred acres of corn that was yet to be harvested. When he suggested that I give cornrow hunting a try, I silently resolved to the likelihood that my pricey out-of-state tag would go unfilled.

Knowing that as an easterner I was inexperienced with hunting in standing corn, my friend gave me a quick overview of how to do it. He said to stand in the open space between the rows, slowly stick my head through between two stalks, and look up and down the next space. If no deer were feeding or bedding in the narrow corridor, I was to step into it and repeat the process in the next row.

"But what about the noise I'll make?"

He laughed and answered, "Believe me, it won't be an issue as long as the wind is up. Just hope it doesn't die down." Wow—was he right.

He dropped me off next to a section of corn that must have been three hundred yards wide and twice as long. As I climbed over the fence and walked toward the wall of stalks, I discovered why the sound of my movements would not be an issue. The relentless wind on the Dakota plains was making every stalk clatter like the tale of an upset timber rattler. The collective sound was huge. I could barely hear myself say out loud, "How cool is this!"

For the next two hours, I had more fun than a kid at a circus as I got amazingly close to both mulies and whitetails that were wide-eyed surprised when I nearly stepped on them. About an hour before sunset, I finally connected with a nice six-by-six that stood still for five seconds too long.

On any other hunt, a strong wind would be a real problem, but that day it provided me with a huge advantage over the keen ears of the deer. So it is with the winds of trouble. Romans 5:3-5 confirms this truth:

> We also exult in our tribulations, knowing that tribulation brings about perseverance; and perseverance, proven character; and proven character, hope; and hope does not disappoint, because the love of God has been poured out within our hearts through the Holy Spirit who was given to us.

In light of these promising verses, I always want to remember that just as the relentless North Dakota winds assisted me in my hunt in the rustling corn, the winds of tribulation often come with spiritual benefits. I hope you'll remember that too.

Father in heaven, it's not in my nature to thank You for tribulation, but I trust You to bring the best from it in my life. I ask for my eyes to be open in the midst of trials so I can see how You are using them to lead me to triumph. In the enduring name of Your Son, amen.

26

The Teacher

What shall we say then? Is the Law sin? May it never be! On the contrary, I would not have come to know sin except through the Law...So then, the Law is holy, and the commandment is holy and righteous and good.

ROMANS 7:7,12

I was at least four hundred yards from where I parked when I realized I had left my headlamp in the bed of my truck. The familiar walk across the open field was easy in the predawn moonlight, but I was about to step into dense woods that would be completely black. Without the lamp, I would have no way of locating the reflector-coated thumbtacks I had placed on tree trunks at eye level to guide me safely and quickly to my deer stand. What to do?

Of course, I did what any adventurous hunter would do. I convinced myself that I could trust my memory and find my way through the dark without the light. And of course, I was wrong.

After stumbling over rotten stumps and freshly fallen limbs, as well as being caught in disgusting and sticky spiderwebs that hadn't been there two weeks earlier, I finally stopped and faced reality. I had no idea where my stand was. I backtracked so I could try again.

At least I thought I did—but ten minutes later I was more confused than ever.

Convinced that it wouldn't be wise to make more deer-disturbing noise by wandering around in the woods, I decided to stand still and simply wait until closer to dawn so I could find my stand. The darkness had taught me one undeniable lesson—I was in need of light.

I could have chosen to be upset with the predawn blackness, but that would have been silly. Nothing is wrong with the darkness that invades the woods. In fact, it serves a good purpose. The critters who forage during the day shift can rest quietly after sundown, and those who feed during the night shift are comfortable hiding in the dark. And the dew that forms overnight gives the thirsty trees and underbrush a needed drink. So for the sake of the earth and its inhabitants, let there be night.

The dark was indeed an effective teacher. And it did more than simply remind me that I needed light as a hunter. It also helped me understand more clearly the value of the Law mentioned in Romans 7. As daunting as God's written Law was, nothing about it was evil. Instead, it served a great purpose. Without the Law, how would men have learned that sin was a major problem? The Ten Commandments served as a tutor, and they still do. To dismiss them and the other commands of God is to ignore the very teacher that can help us understand our need for God's grace and His gift of redemption through Christ.

When the opportunity arises to steal, covet, lie, or commit adultery or any other sin, don't get upset at the voice inside that says, "Don't do it!" Embrace that urging because it's the voice of the Teacher. Otherwise, you'll end up stumbling and tripping, and even worse, you'll never find the peace you long for.

For the record, on the morning of my episode with the forgotten headlamp, letting darkness teach me that I needed the light was a choice that paid off. When dawn finally came, I discovered I was within eyeshot of my stand.

Father and Maker of light, thank You for all Your commandments. They do indeed reveal the sin in me, and they teach me that I have a great need for Your redeeming grace. Praise be to Your name for providing that redemption through Your blessed Son, Jesus, in whose name I pray. Amen.

27

Connections

*I have been crucified with Christ; and it is no longer
I who live, but Christ lives in me; and the life which
I now live in the flesh I live by faith in the Son of
God, who loved me and gave Himself up for me.*

GALATIANS 2:20

If a congregation includes avid deer hunters, something could happen during the sermon that the pastor is not aware of, especially if hunting season is underway. Some of the hunters could be looking right at the preacher and appear to be listening, but in their mind they may be thinking...

I need to move that ladder stand to the east side of the field.

I gotta get some of those expandable broadheads.

I sure hope it's not raining in the morning!

These are only a few examples of the countless images that can consume a hunter's thoughts during a church service. I know because my body has been in a pew when my mind was in the woods. But lest a preacher reads my confession and loses hope that all his study and sermon preparation is for naught when it comes to people like me, I want to offer a word of advice to my fellow distracted hunters.

After feeling ashamed enough times that I let my mind wander the hills during church, I decided to work on my weakness. Over time, and with some conscious effort, I discovered something I could do to stay engaged in the sermon—and make hunting a life-changing spiritual experience as well. I found that I remember scriptural truths more effectively when I link them to hunting experiences. Here's an example.

During a sermon titled "The Grace and Peace of God," our pastor said, "The kind of peace Jesus gives is not the peace we usually long for. We want the kind of peace where there are no problems in our life. Sometimes we think that if we're close enough to God, He will end the conflict around us. But what did He say in John 16:33? 'In the world you have tribulation'! Folks, I want you to understand that the peace Jesus gives is not the absence of conflict; it's the presence of God!"

He paused for a moment to let the wisdom sink in and then said, "It's no accident that Jesus's comment about tribulation was in the context of the coming of the Holy Spirit, who would be our helper. In John 14:16-17, Jesus said, 'I will ask the Father, and He will give you another Helper, that He may be with you forever; that is the Spirit of truth, whom the world cannot receive, because it does not see Him or know Him, but you know Him because He abides with you and will be in you.'"

And here's where our pastor's words connected to my hunter's brain. He said, "Up until the time of Christ's work on the cross, when He suffered a severing of His peace so we could know peace, God's Spirit dwelled *with* man but didn't live *in* man. He couldn't live within us because the sin problem hadn't been dealt with yet. In essence, Jesus was saying, 'Up until this time the Spirit has been *with* you, but now He will be *in* you.'"

At that moment I thought of the fact that when I'm hunting and an animal comes near, it is *with* me in the woods, but it's not *in* me. But because the animal sheds its blood and dies, I can partake of it at the supper table. Then the deer is no longer *with* me, but *in* me. We become one!

When a powerful connection like this is made between the Scriptures and hunting, the truth is forever etched on my heart. And I must say, when I leave church feeling inspired as a follower of Christ and as a hunter too, going back to church and going back into the woods are even more exciting.

If you hunt and/or fish, I appeal to you (for your sake and your pastor's) to listen closely to his sermons. You could make connections that can change your life!

God, I thank You for those who fill the pulpit with Your awesome and enduring truths. I want to be a good listener and receiver of the guidance they offer. And I am especially grateful for those times when a link is made between Your Word and Your great outdoors. You have a marvelous and merciful way of branding Your truth on my heart. Bless the Lord, O my soul!

God willed to make known [to His saints] what is the riches of the glory of this mystery among the Gentiles, which is Christ in you, the hope of glory.

COLOSSIANS 1:27

28

Fear in the Ears

*When Saul and all Israel heard these words of the
Philistine, they were dismayed and greatly afraid.*

1 SAMUEL 17:11

I n the familiar story of David and Goliath, we learn that Saul and
all Israel were gripped with fear merely by *hearing* the giant's ver-
bal taunts. The idea that such dread can come to the heart through
the ears is not lost on me, and here's one reason why.

After graduating from high school, I went to Glenville State
College, located two hours away in the tall hills of central West Virginia. If someone asked me how many miles from home I would be,
I could answer, "It's laundry distance." In other words, I was close
enough to run home on a weekend and "let" my mother wash my
clothes.

The short trip was convenient for laundry service but not for
meeting another real need that I had at the time—to go hunting.
Several weeks had passed since the beginning of the fall semester,
and by late September the gnawing hunger to be in the woods was
fierce. On the Saturdays when I was able to get back home, there
wasn't enough time or daylight to hunt, and Sunday hunting was

out of the question since it was taken up with church, a noon meal with the family, and the return trip to college. Consequently, I was a starving hunter—but all hope was not lost.

The denomination of the church I grew up in had a congregation in the Glenville area that welcomed me. I hadn't attended there long before I started dropping a few hints that I missed hunting back home, and I soon found some fellow hunters in the congregation. By the first of October, my hunting hunger was being fed. I won't forget my first Gilmer County squirrel hunt on some heavily wooded property owned by a man in the church.

Carrying the 12-gauge Remington pump shotgun I brought to college with me (I lived in an apartment, not a dorm—Mama didn't raise no fool!), I headed up the mountainside just after daylight. I found a knee-high oak stump to sit on and settled in to enjoy the morning.

The day began with the temperature around sixty degrees, perfect for an early fall hunt, but by ten o'clock it had warmed to the mid-seventies. Since I hadn't seen any squirrels, I decided to get up and try still hunting for a while. When I stood up to leave, I suddenly heard a sound that I had heard only on TV. My blood instantly ran cold. It was the distinct, loud buzz of a riled-up rattlesnake.

The best I could tell, the noise came from my right and slightly behind me. In that moment I did something I still can't believe I did. Without hesitation and in one fluid series of movements, I removed my gun from my shoulder, gripped it tightly, pushed the safety button to the off position, slid my finger onto the trigger, pointed the barrel just forward of my right boot, and fired all four rounds at the ground in an arc that covered the area where I thought the snake might have been.

When the fifth pumping action and trigger pull yielded a distressing snap of the firing pin, I didn't hang around to see if any of my shots had connected with the slithery beast. Instead, I was

bounding off the mountain even before the report of my Remington died down. The first stride of my departure would probably
have equaled an Olympic long-jump record. I felt like I was airborne for at least five seconds before I landed. I'm as grateful today
for my safe escape as I was that day in the late 1960s, and the incident remains on my top-ten list of most memorable moments in
the woods.

The fear that came with the rattler's warning was instantaneous
and spirit deep. Even the memory of it gives me the heebie-jeebies.
But on the positive side, the unforgettable encounter proves that our
ears can be gates through which fear enters the heart.

In essence, I responded to the rattler's threat by speaking to it—
but I let the Remington do the talking. A shotgun, however, won't
get the job done when we hear, "Your diagnosis is not good," or
"We have to let you go from this job," or "Bring your files to the IRS
office tomorrow." When that happens, what can we do to squelch
the fear? David and Saul can help.

When young David went to the scene of the confrontation
between the Philistines and the Israelites, he arrived just in time to
hear the giant's threats. If he felt any fear, he turned it over to God
so completely that when he saw no one else was willing to take
on Goliath, he stepped up and volunteered for the challenge. Saul
tried to talk him out of it, but David said, "The LORD who delivered
me from the paw of the lion and from the paw of the bear, He will
deliver me from the hand of this Philistine" (1 Samuel 17:37).

David had more words to say when it came time to face the giant.
Fully convinced that God would fight for him and through him, he
dealt with fear by boldly speaking to the source of it.

> You come to me with a sword, a spear, and a javelin, but
> I come to you in the name of the LORD of hosts, the God
> of the armies of Israel, whom you have taunted. This
> day the LORD will deliver you up into my hands, and

I will strike you down and remove your head from you.
And I will give the dead bodies of the army of the Philistines this day to the birds of the sky and the wild beasts
of the earth, that all the earth may know that there is a
God in Israel, and that all this assembly may know that
the LORD does not deliver by sword or by spear; for the
battle is the LORD's and He will give you into our hands
(verses 45-47).

When Saul heard David's confident pronouncement to Goliath, he discovered that just as fear can enter a heart through the ears,
courage can too. Fear is contagious, but so is courage!

Like David, we too can speak to the giants we face, including fear.
And we can rightfully and boldly do it in the name of Jesus, who is
our Savior. Also, just as Saul found courage in David's words, we can
gain courage by hearing and believing that Jesus will speak to our
source of fear the way He did for the disciples who were frightened
by a stormy sea. Mark 4:39 says Jesus "got up, rebuked the wind and
said to the waves, 'Quiet! Be still!' Then the wind died down and it
was completely calm" (NIV).

If you need more courage, let these words of Jesus fill your spiritual ears: "These things I have spoken to you, so that in Me you may
have peace. In the world you have tribulation, but take courage; I
have overcome the world" (John 16:33).

*O Father and my Deliverer, what a blessing to know that You
are the One who goes with me into every battle against the
giant of fear or any other Goliath that would invade my life
and try to destroy me. You alone can bring victory. What a
blessing to know that I can rebuke my foes in Your name and
that You will fill my ears with the hope of Your deliverance as
You speak through Your written Word. Amen.*

Can-Do-It or Conduit

Apart from Me you can do nothing.
JOHN 15:5

There's no way to fully measure the value of having a good, dependable flashlight in my backpack while I'm hunting. The obvious reasons are that it contributes to a safe entrance into the woods in the predawn darkness and a pain-free exit if I fail to leave before the sun fully sets. And of course, when a hunt includes following a blood trail after dark, the bright beam of a flashlight is an absolute must.

These are very good reasons to appreciate such a useful gadget, but there's another reason worth considering. It's an excellent illustration of Jesus's words recorded in John 15:5.

Referring to Himself as the vine and His followers as the branches, Jesus said, "Apart from Me you can do nothing." This bold statement was made clear by the vine-and-branch picture and really needs no further support. But if, like me, you enjoy seeing ancient truths from new angles, take a look at a flashlight.

The hollow cylinder, when empty, is really of no use at all when it comes to supplying light. However, slide a set of batteries inside it, and voilà—let there be rays! If the batteries could talk to the vacant tube, they would say, "Apart from us you can do nothing."

You and I are like an empty flashlight. But unlike a set of batteries that can't speak, our source of power has actually spoken to all of us through His written Word and informed us of an undeniable truth: "Apart from Me you can do nothing."

To put it another way, none of us can spiritually shine on our own. We might like to think that apart from Christ we are *can-do-its*, but according to Jesus, we're not that at all. Instead, we are *conduits* of His light.

Psalm 4:6 asks, "Who will show us any good?" Knowing that humans are incapable of shining the light of God's goodness on our own, the psalmist doesn't linger with an answer. He gives it in the form of a request. "Lift up the light of Your countenance upon us, O Lord!" Note that he said, "*Your* countenance." David recognized that if his life displayed any light at all, it would not be his.

The next time you take out your flashlight, perhaps it will remind you that apart from Christ you can do nothing—especially shine.

Lord Jesus, I read in Matthew 5:16 that You said, "Let your light shine before men in such a way that they may see your good works, and glorify your Father who is in heaven." I truly want this to happen, but I know that any light I have is from You. You are my light, and You will be forever. May You indeed receive all the glory for whatever good is done through me. In the name of Jesus I pray. Amen.

30

He Looked Down

The LORD has looked down from heaven
upon the sons of men
To see if there are any who understand,
Who seek after God.

PSALM 14:2

Some of my most treasured memories of hunting deer from an elevated stand are from times when the wind was in my favor and an unsuspecting whitetail walked in close, stopped, and then looked straight up at me. This is when life is most exciting—at least for a hunter. I don't just *see* the deer's big, dark, nerve-testing eyes; I can *feel* them as they try to process my shape and my out-of-the-ordinary shades of dark and light.

Sometimes the camo pattern on my clothes blends well enough with my surroundings to overcome the educated eyes of a deer. Sometimes not. When I get busted, I always wonder what it was about my appearance the deer didn't like. Was it a movement (even though I thought I was motionless)? Was it alerted by a reflection of light coming from something on me, like the lens of my eyeglasses or my binoculars? I've even wondered if I unknowingly produced a vibe of danger that warned a deer's sixth sense (if deer have one).

The truth is, I'll likely never know exactly why a deer that's not alerted by my scent would choose to run off after looking me over. But what I do know is that when I look below me and stare into the eyes of a mature buck or doe, and it stays relaxed enough not to dart away, that's a very satisfying feeling.

I like to think that the delight I feel when I'm not rejected after being seen by an observant deer under my stand is similar to how God feels when He looks down from heaven and encounters the acceptance of a man or woman. According to the psalmist's words, He looks for those who look for Him. Of course, there's a huge difference between why I look for a deer to come under me and why God looks down at the earth for those who come near Him. My intent for the animal is to take its life. God's intent for the human is to give that person life.

I'm eternally grateful that God granted me the privilege of being among those who have come to Him, looked at Him, found Him acceptable, and been found acceptable in His eyes. I don't even care to imagine what my life would be like otherwise. As the apostle Paul put it, I would be "of all men most miserable" (1 Corinthians 15:19 KJV).

If you're a hunter, maybe sometime in the future you'll be perched in a tree stand and have an encounter with a deer that walks in and looks up at you. If it doesn't snort and run away, and you feel really good about it, may you be reminded that if you look to God and find Him acceptable, He'll look favorably at you as well.

Father in heaven, I give You my deepest thanks for looking down at the earth for those who seek You. I'm one of those who wants to see You, and I trust that You have found me worthy of Your great love, Your amazing grace, and Your boundless mercy. Thank You for giving me abundant life through Your holy Son, Jesus. Blessed be Your name forever and ever. Amen.

31

Angels on Four-Wheelers

Do not neglect to show hospitality to strangers, for by
this some have entertained angels without knowing it.
HEBREWS 13:2

When my son-in-law, Emmitt, and my friend Lindsey arrived at the site where I stood over the 650-pound elk cow that I had taken several minutes earlier, they found me looking worried. Lindsey asked, "Nice cow. Is everything okay?"

I took off my cap and rubbed my head front to back. "Guys, when we headed out here to Colorado, all I had on my mind was the hunt. I didn't think about what had to be done if I got something on the ground. Right now I have two big questions on my mind. One, how do we field dress an elk? And two, how on this green earth are we going to get this beast back to camp? It's on the other side of the ridge and well over a mile away!"

I would rather have heard one of them jokingly say, "What do you mean, 'we'? She's your cow." Instead, both of them just looked at me with an expression that said, "Now we're worried."

For twenty minutes the three of us stood over the huge mound of yet-to-be-deboned meat and rehashed the details of the kill. The conversation was enjoyable, but the truth is, we were just trying to avoid the hard work we had to do and the fact that none of us had field dressed an elk. I had held the back legs of a couple of bulls I took during hunts with a Montana guide, but he performed the duty both times as I watched. Other than that, the biggest critters any of us had ever processed were our Eastern whitetail deer.

Finally I said, "Well, boys, as you know, it's all play before the pull of the trigger and all work afterward. This cow is not going to field dress itself. Time to get busy and find an answer to my first question—how do we do this?"

I dug through my backpack for my knife and elbow-length rubber gloves and then said to Emmitt, "As for how are we going to get this elk back to camp, we're going to need some help. While Lindsey and I carve this cow up, would you mind climbing to the ridgetop and radioing the camp? If you connect with someone, tell them we're going to need some help."

I wasn't sure I was reading him right, but he seemed more than willing to make the strenuous ascent and miss the "major surgery" that was about to happen. I would have felt the same way.

Drawing on what I remembered the Montana guide doing, and with Lindsey holding the legs, I cut and sawed my way to exhaustion. It was a slow, bloody, sweaty process that included an inadvertently punctured paunch, releasing some of the most foul, gag-inducing gut fumes I had ever smelled. Thankfully, the contents of the elk belly didn't contaminate the meat.

It took the better part of an hour for us to complete the job, and as we wrapped the four quarters of elk with cloth, Emmitt returned to the unsightly scene with some good news and bad news.

"I connected with a couple of guys at the camp, and they said they'd bring a truck up to carry the quarters back to camp. However, because this is public land, they can't drive off the road. They can get as far as a parking area down the ridge a ways and meet us there."

I dreaded to ask, but I had no choice: "How close do they think we are to the parking area?"

Having already lifted one of the hind quarters to get an idea of how heavy they were and nearly breaking our backs doing it, both Lindsey and I gasped when Emmitt said, "They figured it's about a mile down the ridge to the west once we get up to the top from here."

I smiled nervously and started singing the words to a song from the '70s: "This'll be the day that I die, this'll be the day that I die."

After a few minutes of saying how sorry we felt for each other that we were about to do the hardest work we could imagine as hunters, we resolved to do what had to be done. Then the unimaginable happened.

It started with a distant *putt-putt* that gradually grew louder. The three of us turned our ears in the direction it was coming from and listened. Lindsey recognized the sound.

"Sounds like a four-wheeler to me."

Emmitt and I agreed and continued to listen. A minute or so later, two four-wheelers appeared above us, heading downhill in our direction. We just stood there speechless as the off-road machines pulled up to where we were.

A man and woman were on one four-wheeler, and a woman was on the second. The man greeted us.

"Got yourselves an elk, I see. That's a lot of meat."

I said, "'Tis indeed. And what are y'all up to today?"

"We're just tooling around. We saw you from the peak behind you and figured you were field dressing something, so we thought we'd come down and see what you got."

"Yes, sir. I filled a cow tag, and the next step is to carry these quarters over to a parking area where some guys from camp are gonna meet us."

As far as I'm concerned, the next words I heard were divine.

"Why don't you let us take it there for you? We know where it is."

I nearly broke my jaws smiling at the man's kind offer. Lindsey and Emmitt were grinning ear to ear too. We loaded up the eighty-pound hindquarters and fifty-pound fronts onto the ATVs, gathered up our gear, and started to fall in behind the machines. Before we did, I asked the strangers if they would show me their backs. They looked puzzled, and the man asked me why. He laughed when I told him.

"Well, sir and ladies, I just want to see what angel wings look like, because I'm quite sure you're heaven-sent."

It may have sounded like I was just enlisting humor as a way of saying thanks to them for their help, but actually I was being serious. Really, I was. What were the chances of not one but two four-wheelers with servant-hearted riders showing up when they did and helping the way they did? Infinitesimal.

I can't say for sure that angels ride four-wheelers. But I have no other explanation for the timing of the help we got on that Colorado mountainside, so maybe they do. If nothing else, the experience increased my faith that God will watch over me and send help when I need it—when I'm hunting and when I'm not.

Thank You, God, for the ways You surprise me with Your helpful intervention. You certainly do make life incredibly exciting. You truly are a good, good Father. Blessed be Your name.

---- (32) ----

A Truth I Can Live With

Behold, You desire truth in the innermost being,
And in the hidden part You will make me know wisdom.
PSALM 51:6

I t's not easy to admit, but in my many years of hunting, I have sometimes wounded an animal and, unfortunately, never found it. However, I can say that because I strive to maintain respect for the life of wild game, I've never given up a search easily. Exhausting all possibilities for recovery is simply the right thing to do.

When I've had to abandon an attempt to retrieve an injured animal, my gut always churns with regret. As I turn back to leave the area, I can't help but imagine the pain the animal may be feeling. The fact that I failed to make a quick and merciful kill follows me out of the woods and haunts me mercilessly.

The remorse has sometimes been so strong that the only way to console myself was to say to myself, *Well, the coyotes have to eat too.*

Why would I come to such a seemingly uncaring conclusion about an animal that I shot and then failed to find? As a matter of confession, very simply, I've said it because I needed a truth I could live with. To think about an animal writhing in pain because of my ineptness produces quite a heavy load of guilt to bear.

On one occasion when I confided in Annie about my tactic for easing the sting of the real truth, she graciously accepted my admission and then got *that* familiar look on her face. It's the expression that lets me know she has a new revelation she is about to share.

Responding to my "It's a truth I can live with" statement, she said, "Now I think I know why some people defend abortion by saying things like, 'A pregnant teen has grim prospects for a future,' 'My body, my right,' 'It's not illegal,' or, 'It's not a baby.' These are truths they can live with. The real truth is too hard to handle."

I was stunned by her insight. It made a lot of sense to me and spurred more conversation about the issue. The more we talked about it, the more we pitied those who were hiding their regret behind a conclusion they felt they could live with.

As we talked, our compassion also extended to those who have had an abortion but have come to understand in their heart of hearts that it was a terribly brutal, God-displeasing thing to do, and who now deal with it by creating a reality they can bear.

People engage in various other immoral activities and create truths they can live with to avoid feelings of guilt. For example, to deal with the gnawing shame that results from committing adultery, a spouse might say, "I don't feel loved at home," or "I'm not appreciated," or "God wants me to be happy."

Adultery is just one of many transgressions that guilty parties try to excuse in such a way. The question each of us should ask ourselves is, *What wrong have I done or am I doing, and what "truth" have I created to justify it?*

Answering that question honestly can be the first step in freedom from the consequences of our wrongdoing. May God give us the courage to be open before Him and to ask Him to be our only

Truth. Because the fact is, He's the only Truth that can set us free from guilt and shame.

> *Father in heaven, I readily admit that I am prone to sin. And like Adam and Eve, I have disobeyed and then defended my actions with a conclusion I can live with. Thank You for Your forgiveness, which reaches even me. Help me to keep an open heart before You. I ask You to be the Truth in my life—THE truth I can live with forever. I ask that this be done to Your glory alone. Amen.*

33

Twin Motivators

*Blessed are those who hunger and thirst for
righteousness, for they will be filled.*

MATTHEW 5:6 NIV

What motivates the average modern American hunter to get
out of a comfortable bed long before sunrise to face the
harsh elements for hours on end? It's rarely our physical hunger or
thirst. Most of us have food and drink in our cupboards and refrig-
erators, and we have reasonable access to grocery stores and restau-
rants. Few of us have to hunt to survive.

Instead, most of us head to the fields and woods because we're
hungry and thirsty for things like these:

friendship

solitude

rest

challenge

escape

spiritual growth

For many hunters, these motivators feel as important as food and water. In fact, if I were asked to put a check mark beside the items that are crucial for me, I could mark them all. The level of hunger and thirst I feel for each one may vary depending on life's circumstances, but hunting always satisfies the cravings.

The fact that I hunt for more reasons than just to nourish my body helps me better understand what Jesus meant when He said, "Blessed are those who hunger and thirst for righteousness, for they shall be satisfied." He didn't say anything about a plate, fork, napkin, entrée, dessert, and coffee. Instead, He mentioned the one thing humans need far more than an earthly meal—righteousness. And not just any righteousness: only His righteousness, which alone can satisfy every hungry seeker.

Jesus used the two words "hunger" and "thirst" together. I've found that if I'm hungry but not thirsty, I can feel okay, or if I'm thirsty but not hungry, I'm still good to go. But when both hunger and thirst are gnawing at me, I'm doubly desperate for food and water.

It's that kind of desire that Jesus referred to when He linked hunger and thirst. On a spiritual level, these are twin motivators that compel a person to long desperately for righteousness. The good news is, when He is allowed to be the One to satisfy the hunger and thirst, it will be fully and eternally fulfilled.

Blessed Savior, thank You for giving me the opportunity to understand what it really means to hunger and thirst for Your righteousness. I eagerly confess that my heart is utterly empty of any good thing. I do so because facing this reality leads me to seek Your presence in my heart. Come and be that which satisfies my hunger and thirst. In Your name, amen.

34

The Double-Edged Question

*For we are God's handiwork, created in
Christ Jesus to do good works, which God
prepared in advance for us to do.*

Ephesians 2:10 niv

My wife's late parents, N.R. and Sylvia Williamson, raised six children. Part of their parenting experience took place during the turbulent '60s. At that time, many of the youth of our nation, including some of the Williamson kids, were asking a two-part question: "Who am I, and why am I here?"

Mrs. Williamson knew well that this question wasn't new, but had been around through the ages. It was a legitimate inquiry by people who wanted to clearly understand their roots and the purpose for their existence. However, she felt as if the two-part question didn't point to an honest longing to know the meaning of life. Rather, it opened the door to all manner of spiritual confusion, including mysticism and humanism.

After hearing her children ask such a "deep" question more times than she thought was good for them, she decided to provide an answer. Her intent was not only to bring clarity of identity and purpose to her young seekers of truth but also to bring a screeching halt to the philosophical distraction that was stealing her children's attention and keeping them from focusing on their chores around the dairy farm.

With those goals in mind, she was ready whenever one of them would mournfully ask, "Who am I, and why am I here?" Without missing a beat while peeling potatoes or kneading biscuit dough, she'd say, "Child, let me take you down to the courthouse. That's where you'll find out who you are. As for why you're here, you'll have to figure that out on your own!" Enough said.

The Williamson kids were blessed to have a mother who was wise enough to recognize the misleading intent of their question. To her kids' benefit, she was also brave enough to offer them a common-sense answer. Her response contained a bit of humor, but it also served as a serious defense against the spirit of confusion that would have invaded her offspring. As it turned out, all six of the Williamson children grew to be as perceptive as their mother and able to repel other questions and attitudes that may have led toward vain thinking.

Mrs. Williamson's astute response to the double-edged question not only bore good fruit in her children's lives but also inspired me as the dad of two children as I tried to guide them to a right understanding of their roots and their purpose. As for the "who am I" part of the question, it was easy to help them accept the fact that they were Chapmans with Williamson blood. They have no doubt about that detail, because Annie and I went out of our way to make many long round trips from Tennessee to West Virginia so they could connect with their roots.

When it came to helping our children see their purpose in life, we often reminded them that according to Ephesians 2:10, God had prepared the works they were to do long before they were born. We took great delight in helping them explore various interests, such as history, art, music, sports, teaching, and economics. In due time, both our son and daughter settled into what they feel is their reason for being here. And if you ask them, they both would answer in order of importance: to glorify their Creator, to be faithful spouses, and to be parents who can guide their own children to a relationship with God.

Beyond those purposes, our son would likely say he is to make the best music he can possibly make so God will be honored by excellence. Our daughter would likely say she wants to paint the Spirit and love of God onto every canvas she works with. Needless to say, Annie and I are quite proud of our children, and we're very grateful they know who they are and why they're here.

While elk hunting in Colorado, I thought about Mrs. Williamson's homespun and effective response to her children's double-edged question and its positive effect on my own family. The combination of memories came to mind while I sat quietly one morning in the shadow of a scrub oak, waiting and hoping to see a bull appear below me at a watering hole in a sun-filled draw.

The chilly October weather had already caused the leaves to turn brown and begin to fall, and as if cued by an unheard voice, one of the leaves fell into my lap. I picked it up, stared at it for a few seconds, and then realized that every leaf on every tree had a reason to exist. Then I thought of the fact that each person in my family has a purpose, a work to do that was prearranged before any of us were formed in the womb.

My prayer is that each of us will let God our Great Guide reveal to us what that work is, just as Mrs. Williamson encouraged her kids to do. May it also be true for you and those you love.

Life Goes Around

I'm a leaf on a tree on a Colorado mountain
Just one among the millions, but who's countin'

I'll do my part in my Maker's work of art
I'll hang on
Till my summer is gone
Then I'll fall to the ground
Life goes around

I'm a drop of morning dew on a white rhododendron
That grows along the trail they call the Appalachian
I was made for this hour to give a drink to this flower
I am here
Then like a goodbye tear
I'll fall to the ground
Life goes around

Everything God made
Has something good to give
Every soul by His grace
Has a reason and a purpose to live
Then we fall to the ground
Life goes around

I'm a grain of sand and I was chosen
To take my place on a beach by an ocean
Where a child comes to play on a blue-sky day
For a while
I'm in his hand
I'll make him smile
Then I'll fall to the ground
Life goes around[6]

O Father in heaven, You are indeed my wonderful Creator. Because You made me, You surely know the works I am to do while I walk the trail of time. I ask You to reveal and confirm my purpose for taking part in life. And if my work needs to change as time goes on, help me to recognize and follow Your guidance. Simply, I long to do Your will, for I know if I walk in it, the path will lead me to my eternal home in the place You have prepared for those who faithfully follow You. I ask that this be done to Your glory alone. In Christ's name, amen.

35

No Eating

The LORD God commanded the man, saying,
"From any tree of the garden you may eat
freely; but from the tree of the knowledge of
good and evil you shall not eat, for in the day
that you eat from it you will surely die."

GENESIS 2:16-17

I once thought a No Hunting sign was the most insulting, frustrating, cruel, and unusually punishing thing I'd ever seen in God's great outdoors. My argument was that the planet belongs to all of mankind, and ownership of little sections of it by anyone was wrong. Of course, the reason I thought that way was that I had seen a trophy deer or a huge "long beard" on a great piece of property I couldn't hunt on due to someone having the audacity to hang those stupid signs all around the perimeter of their personal paradise. Unfair!

I was younger then, so I'd prefer to blame my "what's theirs is mine" attitude on immaturity. But I now know the real reason I wanted to hunt where I couldn't hunt. It wasn't because of my *youthful* nature, but rather my *sinful* nature. The deal is, I'm a son of Adam, and sadly, I possess a propensity for disobeying the "You're

Not Allowed to Have This" signs. I felt that way back then—and, admittedly, sometimes I still do. But there's a really good reason not to yield to those feelings, and it has its roots in the book of Genesis.

Most of us know that in the Garden of Eden, the devil convinced Adam and Eve that God was withholding something of great value from them by saying they could eat from every tree except the tree of the knowledge of good and evil. They believed the devil's lie, which led them to shameful disobedience and an eventual forced exit from their beautiful home.

Our ancient parents didn't realize that God wasn't withholding something from them. Rather, He was giving them the one thing they needed most. He was providing them the opportunity to trust that His ways are best and that obedience to His commands would be their most valuable source of knowledge. As it turns out, putting up a No Eating sign, so to speak, was not the worst thing God did to the original couple, as the devil led them to believe. It was the greatest good He did for them.

When a landowner puts up a No Hunting sign, he probably has no idea what an opportunity he is offering to hunters who want to be God-followers. It provides us a chance to prove that our greatest desire is the same as the apostle Paul's, who said in 2 Corinthians 5:9, "We also have as our ambition, whether at home or absent [or in the woods], to be pleasing to Him."

Father, I admit that it's not always easy to say no to my fleshly desires, but You know I want to refuse them. I realize that in the woods of this life, there are a lot more signs to obey than just No Hunting, including No Committing Adultery, No Stealing, No Gossiping, No Fishing, and many more. I want my chief ambition to be to please You by trusting that Your ways are higher and better than my ways and by obeying Your marvelous commands, which keep me wise and spiritually alive and safe. Thank You for Your love for me that's revealed in things like a No Hunting sign. You truly are a kind and caring Father. Amen.

36

Hit the Lynch

He shall speak for you to the people; and he will be
as a mouth for you and you will be as God to him.

Exodus 4:16

I am delighted and amazed when a scene in the Bible comes alive in a hunting situation. When it does, the biblical meaning becomes clearer as if I were turning the adjustment rings on a pair of binoculars for an in-focus view. For example, consider the turkey calls my buddy Lindsey and I carry with us during spring gobbler season.

Most of the calls are good enough to get by, but one of them is a yelp-and-cluck above all others. There's no way to number the times we've been out chasing toms, and while "walkin' and talkin'" (our description of covering ground and stopping occasionally to call and try to get a gobbler to yell back at us), I'll say, "Let's stop here and go ahead and hit the Lynch."

"Lynch" comes from the brand name printed on the top of a sliding paddle attached to a box. When the chalked underside of the paddle scrapes across one of the two thin walls of the box, the call speaks more like a hen than any other I've heard. Lindsey has had it for years, and it only gets better with time. The raspy tone of the yelps has fooled more curious (and "love starved") toms than you can shake a shotgun at.

The reason the Lynch is so valuable and well used is that it talks turkey far better than either of us can. When I'm hunting alone, I have no choice but to try a call from my collection of slate pots, push/pull types, and diaphragm calls. But if the two us of are hunting together, to put our best cluck forward, it's always "Lindsey, hit the Lynch."

I see a connection between the Lynch and the well-known story of Moses in Exodus 4. Moses felt terribly inept at communication, so he decided he needed a mouth to speak for him. God honored his appeal to have someone act as his spokesman. Enter Aaron.

The Scriptures say Moses was not *the* God of Aaron, but he was *as* God to Aaron. Moses received the words, but Aaron would be his mouth. They became a team for the sake of guiding the Israelites on their exodus from Egypt.

Moses knew what God wanted him to say but couldn't do it very well without Aaron. And Lindsey and I know what we want to communicate with turkeys, but we have to lean on a call like the Lynch to get the message across.

Moses was willing to let Aaron speak for him, and Lindsey and I have decided to let the Lynch do the turkey talking for us. This comparison not only makes the biblical account come alive but also helps us as songwriters. Here's how.

Lindsey and I have written many songs together and pitched them to other artists to record. Usually we sing them ourselves on the demo recording, but occasionally we agree that the song needs a different voice, and we hire a professional singer. Our egos are not damaged when we enlist the services of another voice, because our goal is to make the song the best it can be. Besides, if Moses was willing to give Aaron the responsibility of communicating what God wanted him to say, we can feel good about hiring an "Aaron," or a "Lynch," you might say, to come to the studio and sing for us.

If you're a hunter who uses a tried-and-true game call, be it a turkey, deer, elk, duck, or any other type, may it always remind you that you're illustrating an unforgettable story in the Word of God. And if you ever have to enlist the voice of someone to speak on your behalf, remember Aaron, or if it helps, remember these words: "Hit the Lynch!"

> *Father in heaven, how grateful I am that You reveal Your wisdom to me in every aspect of life—including hunting. I pray that you will open my eyes to even more life-changing truths when I'm enjoying Your great outdoors. To Your glory and for the sake of growing in Your ways, I ask this in the name of Jesus. Amen.*

37

Here and There

We are no longer to be children, tossed here and there by
waves and carried about by every wind of doctrine, by
the trickery of men, by craftiness in deceitful scheming.

EPHESIANS 4:14

I've never been dangerously tossed about on the waves of an angry sea like many have, but I did have an inland experience that I can say was somewhat similar. It helped me better appreciate the apostle Paul's admonition not to be tossed here and there. The encounter happened in a tree stand my friend mounted with great effort and graciously invited me to use.

Following his detailed directions, I managed to find the tall, straight tree that held the stand. I stood at the base of it and visually followed the staggered metal steps up the trunk, and I couldn't believe what I saw. The platform looked small, and for a good reason. It wasn't that far from the clouds in my opinion. I guessed that it was at least thirty feet off the ground, and I thought, *Maybe my friend has a death wish for himself—or me.*

I wondered how I could possibly feel comfortable and enjoy the hunt so far above the earth. I kept thinking about the old adage that says falling doesn't hurt, but the sudden stop can be painful. I certainly didn't want to prove it true. But for a reason I can't explain other than a propensity for adventure, I decided to reach into my psyche for some bravery and give the mile-high seat a try.

The scariest part of the process was stepping off the foot spikes onto the stand. It required a slight swing of my body to get one foot on the platform as I held on to the trunk with both arms. I was literally shaking when I got both feet on the stand. Still hugging the tree tightly, I finally found the nerve to carefully turn around and sit down on the cushioned seat. I debated looking down, and when I finally did, I said out loud, "This is nuts!"

I put on the safety harness that was left for me to use and sat motionless for half a minute, trying to adjust to my lofty surroundings. After settling in and feeling more confident, I was able to relax a bit and enjoy the hunt. All was going great—until the wind picked up and the tree began to sway a little. At first it was a gentle lean from side to side. But the weather deteriorated, and within ten minutes the once tolerable sway became a wild ride.

Longing to feel safe again, and trying not to imagine the tree falling with me in it, I decided to head back to earth. My legs were wobbly when I got to the ground. I felt as unsteady as I ever had. I later thanked my friend for the use of his stand but vowed I'd never use it again. However, I did promise to pray for him as he used it.

Looking back, I realize that the most dangerous part of the experience was the severe "here and there" of the tree trunk in the strong wind. I could have been thrown out and maimed or killed. It was indeed a real-life illustration of how my spiritual life can suffer if I let myself be tossed here and there by the winds of man-made doctrine and deceitful teaching.

The answer to avoiding injury in a too-tall tree stand is simply to lock on to the thicker, stabler section of the trunk. In a similar way, to avoid getting hurt by "every wind of doctrine," it's wise to carefully examine God's written Word, attach to the meaty truths in it, and be fixed in what I believe. Then, when (not if) the strong winds of deception begin to blow, I won't get hurt by the peace-stealing, doubt-inducing, confidence-killing "here and there" effect it can have on my heart. May it be so for me—and for you too.

Jesus, thank You that Your teaching is trustworthy, solid, and without trickery. Help me find spiritual stability as I study Your words, Your ways, and Your wisdom, which can deliver me from being confused and destroyed by the vicious winds of unsound teaching. You know I don't want to be spiritually inflexible, that I want to be willing to be moved to a new place where Your truth is leading, but please help me not to be tossed around by the deceptions of men whose goal is to lead me astray. In Your name I pray. Amen.

38

The Third Question

*Make sure that your character is free from the
love of money, being content with what you
have; for He Himself has said, "I will never
desert you, nor will I ever forsake you."*
HEBREWS 13:5

I've always wondered if *contentment* and *wanting* can coexist in a person's life. Or are they mutually exclusive? When the Bible advises me to be content, does it mean I should abandon my longing for something that might make life better or more enjoyable? For example, if I am content to fish from my canoe with its trolling motor, does that mean I won't want an eighteen-foot fiberglass bass boat with a 250-horsepower outboard motor, a four-blade stainless steel prop, front and rear depth finders, and an extra-large live well? Hmm...what to do?

Perhaps my detailed description of the dream bass boat shows that I've wrestled with wanting. You better believe I'd like to have a shiny new gas-powered water toy that would scream across the lake at sixty miles per hour to the next fishing hole instead of my plastic canoe and battery-powered trolling motor. But for now it's a fantasy—though one I enjoy having.

Here's why I've yet to make the plunge for a big bass boat. It's not that my credit history is bad and I couldn't cover the monthly outlay. Instead, I've chosen to make an item like this a matter of prayer. This has been my preferred policy since the day I heard the following wisdom. I don't remember who provided it, but I'll be forever grateful for it.

Before making a purchase, we can ask ourselves two questions. One question will help us follow God without being encumbered by the things of this world. The other one won't.

The unhelpful question is, can I afford it?

If this is how we make our choice, then the deciding factor is money, which the King James Version calls "mammon." Jesus warned against using this as the basis of our spending decisions: "Ye cannot serve God and mammon" (Matthew 6:24).

The helpful question is, does God want me to have it?

This question turns our heart away from serving mammon to serving God. When we ask this question, wait patiently for the answer, and abide by it (whether it's a yes or no), we spare ourselves a lot of financial trouble.

Seeking God about spending is simply the wise thing to do. It's not always the fun way, because when we long for something, our flesh doesn't like the word "no." But our willing obedience to the Lord always gratifies the Spirit. I prefer to trust that if I've prayed about an item and I sense that God wants me to have it, He will provide the means to get it. And if I get it, having it is never a burden.

If you desire something right now but are asking the wrong question, maybe this lyrical look at the value of contentment will help you ask the right question.

Real Good Life

I was fishing one day on the riverbank
In the morning shade of a willow tree

Had a few on the stringer, it was time to go
A stranger in a suit stopped and said to me

"Looks like you did good. Been fishing long?"
I said, "Just a little while, but now I'm through."
He said, "You got a lot of time left in your day
What do you plan to do?"

I said, "I'm gonna head on home, spend time with the
     kids
Call a few friends over, cook 'em up some fish
Then sit down and talk with my sweet wife
And thank God above for a real good life"

The man said, "Good as you fish, here's what you ought
     to do
Take out a loan, buy a fishing boat
With your good skills, you could pay it off quick
Buy a few more, make the business grow
In twenty years' time you could sell it all
You'd be a wealthy man, you'd have it made
You could come back here when the deal is done
And fish all day in this willow shade"

I said, "Sir, if you will, help me get this straight
If I follow your plan, and do it your way
I'd be gone from home for twenty years
Make a lot of money, then come back here
But would I have a home? Would I know my kids?
Would I still have friends to cook 'em up some fish?
Would I be a stranger to my dear wife?
Could I still say it's a real good life?"

He looked long at me, then he said
"I'm glad I stopped, but I gotta go."
He turned to leave, then turned back around
And said, "I just thought you'd like to know

I'm gonna head on home, spend time with the kids
Call a few friends over, cook 'em up some fish

Then sit down and talk with my sweet wife
And thank God above for a real good life"[7]

Lord, help me to ask the right question when it comes to acquiring things. Then help me to clearly hear Your response and be willing to live by it. For the sake of living content in this world so that my life brings glory to You, amen.

39

The Indoorsman

*I have no greater joy than this, to hear of
my children walking in the truth.*

3 John 4

I've been asked on several occasions if I grew up hunting with my
dad. Those who assume my late father introduced me to the great
outdoors usually seem surprised when I answer no. Before they can
hide their shock, I quickly add, "Dad wasn't a hunter, he was a fisherman—of men! He loved to preach."

What a blessing it was to be the son of a man who possessed a
huge passion for baiting a "sermon hook" with the gospel of Christ
and dropping it into the waters that held the spiritually hopeless.
Even as a child and teenager, I could see he was happiest when
he was used by the Lord to reel someone into His family with his
preaching or to help a struggling believer grow in the faith by hearing the Word.

I never felt shortchanged by Dad's lack of interest in the outdoors, and I still don't. I would have been a fool to resent his passion for leading lost souls to Christ. And when a man who attended
the church he pastored introduced me to hunting, I never sensed

that Dad resented the close friendship that developed between me and my outdoor mentor. It was a freedom that made me respect my dad even more.

Dad is now in heaven. From time to time I'll hear and see things that remind me of him. The sight of his well-used Bible (which my mother uses), the sound of one of his favorite gospel songs on the radio, his hammer in my toolbox, and sometimes the way I use my hands are just a few things that bring sweet memories of him. But one of my favorite reminders of my dad was recently triggered by what I heard in the pulpit at the church Annie and I attend.

It was probably the fourth or fifth Sunday after we became regular members that I heard our pastor say something that made me smile and made my appreciation for him skyrocket. As he opened his sermon, he said something like this: "Y'all know that I'm from Alabama, home of the Crimson Tide—but I don't like football. I don't watch it. And Talladega Superspeedway is in Alabama, but I don't watch NASCAR. I'm not a fan of golf, I don't hunt, I don't fish, and my greatest fear is swimming in the ocean where there are sharks."

I'm not sure what point he went on to make with his candid statement, because in that moment I was caught up in the thought, *Yep. I've come full circle. I'm now back under the pastoring of my non-outdoor dad!* For a few seconds, our preacher disappeared in my imagination and was replaced by Pastor Paul Chapman. I could see Dad's snow-white hair. He looked distinguished in his coat and tie, and I could hear him reading his sermon Scripture text from his leather-bound King James Version of the Bible. It was an incredibly happy moment for me. I thought, *I really am at my home church!*

I'm fortunate to have the background of my "I'd rather be fishing for men" pastor-dad to help me be so accepting of a shepherd who is admittedly not an avid fan of the outdoors. Of course, not everyone has that advantage. Some have a non-hunting, non-sports-minded pastor, and they struggle with giving him their attention and respect. If that's the case for you, I hope you'll come to realize what a tremendous spiritual deficit you might have suffered if your preacher's greatest joy was not found in helping you walk in truth. Maybe it's time to count your blessings and see what a gift God has given you in your indoorsman pastor.

Father in heaven, what a great blessing You have given in pastors whose chief passion is to lead Your people in truth and to reach out with Your message of hope to those who are yet to know Your marvelous redemption. I pray for them now, that You will keep them and those they love in Your good care as they do Your work on our behalf. In Christ's name, amen.

He Loves to Preach

For our pastor on his fiftieth birthday

Pastor Brad was born in Alabam
And from what we understand
There's not a drop of Crimson Tide in his blood
He's never even liked the game
In fact he thinks it's quite insane
To sit and watch those boys fight and shove

If you want to see him get teed off
Ask him what he thinks of golf
He don't want to waste his time with barnyard pool
He don't hunt and he don't fish
Never watches NASCAR on his dish
But that's all right 'cause we still think he's cool

'Cause he loves to preach about the cross
He loves to help a sinner realize he's lost
It's in his smile it's plain to see
There's nothing he likes more than feedin' sheep

We thank God, yes, we thank God
He loves to preach

And you won't find him having fun
On an ocean beach in the sun
He'll tell you it's the last thing on his heart
He's says as far as he can tell
The only thing that rivals hell
Is going out and swimming with the sharks

But he loves to preach about the cross
He loves to help a sinner realize he's lost
It's in his smile it's plain to see
There's nothing he likes more than feedin' sheep
We thank God, yes, we thank God
He loves to preach
We thank God 'cause we love to eat
And he loves to preach[8]

40

In Season and out of Season

I solemnly charge you in the presence of God and of
Christ Jesus, who is to judge the living and the dead,
and by His appearing and His kingdom: preach the
word; be ready in season and out of season; reprove,
rebuke, exhort, with great patience and instruction.

2 TIMOTHY 4:1-2

When serious hunters and anglers hear the word "season," their first thought could very well be, *Which one?* Is it spring gobbler, crappie, walleye, deer, elk, bear, goat, ram, salmon, trout, duck, bow, gun, muzzleloader, juvenile? We need clarification, please!

I admit that I am among those who are prone to filter words through the mesh of my camo face mask or my minnow net. It's a tendency I deal with even when I'm reading the Bible. For example, even though I'm well aware that Paul was not referring to the hunting or fishing calendar when he said to Timothy, "Be ready in season and out of season," I think of the woods or a body of water when I read or hear the verse.

So, what did Paul mean by "be ready in season and out of season"?

The answer is, he was addressing the matter of convenience when it comes to telling others about Christ. The International Standard Version offers this translation: "Be ready to do this whether or not the time is convenient."

If anyone appreciates doing something of importance regardless of whether it's convenient, hunters and anglers do. Rain, wind, snow, hot sun, extremely early and late hours—none of these conditions keep us from doing what we long to do. Come what may, we're ready to hit the trail whenever a season is in. It's an attitude of determination that would serve the message of the gospel well. It would help especially when we face such adversities as the rain of ridicule, the powerful winds of evildoers, or the intense heat of mockers. If we truly want to share the hope of Christ with others, none of these concerns can stop us when soul-winning season is in.

God, thank You for speaking Your heart to me with words that catch my outdoor ear. You are indeed worthy of sharing with others whether it's convenient or not. I ask for Your courage to be in me whenever the opportunity arises to make You known to the lost. Blessed be Your name forever. Amen.

41

Treasures in a Plowed Field

*The sorrow that is according to the will of God produces
a repentance without regret, leading to salvation.*
2 Corinthians 7:10

I t was nearing the noon hour, and the warm mid-April breeze felt glorious on my face as I stood in the shadow of a huge oak at the eastern edge of a long, freshly plowed field. Turkey season had been underway for two weeks. On a couple of previous trips to this farm, I had heard some gobblers but hadn't seen them. The memory of their thundering yells was all I had taken home, but I wasn't bummed. Instead, the sound assured me there were birds in the area, and my hopes for a face-to-beak meeting were high.

After a full morning of waiting, walking, and occasionally calling with no responses from the male birds, I enjoyed a break by taking in an energy-boosting half bottle of vitamin water and a granola bar. As I chomped on a bite of the crunchy treat, I thought I heard what I was hoping to hear. I paused mid-chew and listened intently. He bellowed again, and I swallowed hard. The sound seemed to come from a meadow on the other side of the woods at the western end of the field. It was time to end my snack and continue the hunt.

I was confident the timber between the gobbler and myself was dense enough to hide me as I walked across the open field. But as I stepped into the recently upturned dirt, I immediately realized I had a problem.

After the field had been plowed, rain had washed the dirt off the small rocks in the top layer of soil. Some of the fragments captured my attention. It was *flint*. Why was seeing flint a problem? The answer is—arrowheads.

Hardly anything is more fascinating to me than finding a piece of the distant past in a piece of flint that was skillfully shaped into an arrowhead. Kneeling down and slowly removing an arrowhead from the dirt always makes me feel mysteriously connected to the ancient soul who formed it and used it. On the rare occasions when I find one of the stony treasures, I pause, close my eyes, grip it tightly in my hand, and wonder, *What did the person who used this tool look like? What was their name? What was their life like?* Knowing that centuries may have passed since a human had touched the precious stone adds to the emotion of the discovery.

Seeing flicks of flint in the dirt that day was a problem because I was instantly tempted to abandon my hunt and instead spend the remainder of my time scouring the field for arrowheads. But before I gave in to the idea, I realized I could do both. So I hurried across the field while carefully watching where I stepped to avoid reburying even the tiniest piece of shiny flint under my boots. My plan was to continue pursuing the gobbler and return to the field later.

By the time I got through the patch of woods far enough to see the meadow, it was empty and quiet. I called several times in the next forty-five minutes with no response. The sting of disappointment I felt for having been snookered again by the woods-wise bird was eased by two thoughts. One, I knew I could come back in a couple of days and try again, and two, I still had about an hour to spend in the flint-peppered field I had just walked through.

Past successful experiences with arrowhead hunting made the search doubly exciting. Just the anticipation of seeing a serrated, pointed tip peeking through the dirt, pinching it between my thumb and forefinger, and slowly lifting it out of its age-old grave had been thrilling before. If it happened this day, I wouldn't know until it was fully removed if it would be a broken fragment or the entire arrowhead. Either way it would be a treasure. Then there was the exhilarating possibility of seeing an entire arrowhead just lying there, shining in the sun, waiting to be found. The very thought kept my eyes fixed intently on the ground.

That day I did manage to find one nearly complete arrowhead to add to my collection. I considered it a real prize, but it wasn't all I found of value. As I quietly searched the tilled soil, I reflected on the reason why the arrowheads were visible—the winter-hardened, undisturbed ground had been turned with a plow. I realized I was walking through a picture of what can happen when God turns the soil of our souls. That process can be painful, but it can reveal spiritual treasures that otherwise would never have been known.

Perhaps the most profound and life-changing example of this kind of discovery is what can be uncovered when the sharp edge of guilty sorrow cuts through a person's heart after they've done someone wrong. When the response to the sorrow produces an apology, there's a priceless treasure that may not have been found had the soil of the offender's heart not been tilled by sorrow. It's called "reconciliation."

Second Corinthians 7:10 refers to reconciliation regarding our relationship with our Creator God. When "sorrow that is according to the will of God produces a repentance" in a sinner's heart, the renewed fellowship that person finds with God is immeasurably priceless. It's sort of like finding a fully intact, flawless flint arrowhead in a freshly plowed field. May God help us all discover that kind of joy.

Father in heaven, thank You from the depths of my being for those times when the ground of my heart has been cut by the plow of godly sorrow—the kind that leads me to ask for Your forgiveness. I admit that those painful times of repentance have revealed the treasure of Your pardon. I know there's nothing on earth I could hold in my hand that would be more valuable or that could cause me to feel more connected to You. Blessed be Your name forever. Amen.

Quick Change

*As he was traveling, it happened that he was approaching
Damascus, and suddenly a light from heaven flashed
around him; and he fell to the ground and heard
a voice saying to him, "Saul, Saul, why are you
persecuting Me?" And he said, "Who are You, Lord?"
And He said, "I am Jesus whom you are persecuting."*

Acts 9:3-5

Saul's blinding-light conversion experience as told in Acts 9 is an astounding story. It's simply amazing to think that in one moment he was one type of person, and in the next he was someone totally different.

On a morning bowhunt a few years ago, I got a glimpse of how instantaneous a change of heart can be. I had been self-filming hunts for a couple of seasons using a small digital camera mounted to my bow. I already had a few exciting doe kills in the video archives, so I hoped to capture the taking of a buck so I could add it to a mix of clips I would show at upcoming wild-game dinners.

When there was just enough light to see about fifty yards into the cut soybean field I was watching from my makeshift ground blind, I saw the silhouette of a deer slowly moving left to right. It appeared to be a male, but the mist was too thick for me to be positive. I slowly raised my binoculars to my eyes to get a better look and got really excited when I saw the deer's sizable rack.

I carefully and quietly dug for my grunt call in my daypack, put it to my lips, and gave it a couple of short blows. Forty-five seconds later I was being approached by a soon-to-be star in my homemade movie.

I pressed the record button on the camera, but it felt like I didn't press hard enough, so I pressed it again. Then I attached my release to the bowstring. When I looked up, the buck was within twenty yards of me. He turned his head to look back, and I took the opportunity to come to full draw.

I'm not sure how much time passed as I held the string back, but my arms were getting weak. I glanced at the camera monitor and saw the buck in the center of the frame standing broadside. I put my eye back to the sight pins, placed the green, twenty-yard dot on his shoulder, and pressed the release trigger.

The arrow launch sounded loud in the extreme quiet of the windless morning, and then I heard the thud of the arrow impacting the buck's lung area. I kept the bow up and immediately looked at the camera monitor. Keeping him center-frame as he bounded back in the direction he came from, I filmed his run until he stopped. He stood in that spot for about five seconds, began to weave, and then simply fell over. I didn't want to make the video bounce, so I had to force myself not to celebrate with some vigorous leg pounding.

My first words after seeing the deer expire on camera were, "This is going to be awesome footage for the next event!" But elation turned instantly to deflation when I looked closer at the monitor. Instead of a red flashing dot indicating that the camera was in record mode, I saw a green dot and two green bars. My heart sank with the realization that the camera had been in pause mode the entire time. I didn't get a single frame of the kill.

Feeling certain the buck was deceased, I quickly checked to see if I was wrong about not getting the shot on video. I wasn't wrong. It didn't take long to figure out that my first push of the record button had actually started the recording, but the second push put the camera back in pause mode. I was sick with regret, and for the next few minutes I just sat there, falling deeper into despair. Then, almost as if someone said it aloud, I heard something that shook me to the core.

You're more concerned about not getting the footage than you are about taking the life of an animal. Where's your respect for the deer?

I can't explain how depressed I suddenly felt in that moment. Knowing that I had put more value on commercialism than on creation made me sad to the core. I tried to dismiss the sorrow, but it wouldn't go away. I finally looked across the field toward the dead deer and apologized. Then I did something I never dreamed I would do.

I closed the monitor door on the camera, detached it from the shelf it rested on, and removed the shelf from the bow. I did so with the intention of never self-filming another hunt. My decision was to return to hunting only for the purpose of sustenance. I won't condemn anyone who wants to film me while I hunt, or any other hunter for that matter, but I decided then and there that I would not let technology distract me from maintaining the respect I want to feel for the lives of the animals I take.

In no way do I equate what happened that morning with a spiritual conversion, but it helped me understand how quickly a person can change. I immediately turned away from one reason for hunting and turned toward another motivation. As a result, I can better understand Saul's instantaneous transformation on the road to Damascus.

If Paul had written the song "Amazing Grace," his version might have been, "I once could see but now I'm blind," and he would have considered that his greatest blessing. The shift he made in a brief time from being a sighted enemy of God to being His blinded servant was indeed astoundingly quick. But in reality, something similar happens to anyone today who yields their life to Christ. There's just one difference.

A new convert who encounters and embraces the light of Christ goes immediately from the sad state of being spiritually blinded by sin to the rapturous joy of being spiritually sighted by His grace. It's a quick change that makes the heart able and more than willing to sing, "I was blind but now I see." I'm thankful I can sing those words. I hope you can too!

Father, thank You for the miraculous way You can instantly bring a person out of darkness into light. Truly, Your grace is amazing. Blessed be Your holy name! Amen.

Moments of Heaven

If I go and prepare a place for you, I will
come again and receive you to Myself, that
where I am, there you may be also.

JOHN 14:3

Heaven—just the word brings a sense of calm, a feeling of peace, and a certain hope for an existence without trouble or pain. What a wonderful gift of a hopeful future God has given all who trust in Him.

Looking forward to eternity with God in the place He has already prepared for us indeed brings a joy beyond describing. Yet every once in a while God grants us a tiny glimpse of what it will be like in "the sweet by and by." And in my experience, many of those precious peeks into what awaits us have happened while in God's great outdoors. Here is a list of a few that I've enjoyed.

Moments of Heaven

Morning sun on a mountain snow
Paints the world with a golden glow
Bluebird singing in a meadow green

Feeling the freedom in his wings
These are...

Moments of heaven here on the earth
No way to measure what they are worth
Praise to the Father for the joy He has given
To be touched now and then by moments of heaven

Gentle breeze, cottonwood shade
Cools the skin on a July day
Children laughing, running in the park
Not a single worry in their hearts
These are...

Moments of heaven here on the earth
No way to measure what they are worth
Praise to the Father for the joy He has given
To be touched now and then by moments of heaven

Family table, breaking bread
Love and peace in every word that's said
Someone's missing, been gone too long
Look down the road and see them coming home
These are...

Moments of heaven here on the earth
No way to measure what they are worth
Praise to the Father for the joy He has given
To be touched now and then by moments of heaven[9]

How grateful I am, O God, for the hope of heaven. When the road of this life gets rough and steep, it is truly a comfort to remember that we can find rest by following You to Your place. And how utterly thankful I am for those moments here on earth when You let me sample a mere second of what eternity with You will be like. Until I'm there, lead me on here in Your grace and in Your redeeming righteousness. In Christ's name, amen.

He will wipe away every tear from their eyes,
and death shall be no more, neither shall there
be mourning, nor crying, nor pain anymore,
for the former things have passed away.

REVELATION 21:4 ESV

---(44)---

Breaking News

The righteous man perishes,
and no man takes it to heart;
And devout men are taken away,
while no one understands.
For the righteous man is taken away from evil,
He enters into peace;
They rest in their beds,
Each one who walked in his upright way.

Isaiah 57:1-2

One of the benefits of going to the woods and the fields to hunt or to the water to fish is getting away from the news for a little while. I don't know how everyone else feels these days about the constant hammering of reports about all the chaos going on in the world, but I for one am wearied by it.

One of my least favorite lines to hear on TV is, "We start with BREAKING NEWS!" When I hear it I usually respond, "No! Give me a *break*—the news is on!" I know that leading with a shock phrase is a broadcasting tactic networks use to grab my attention and keep me on the couch long enough to see their commercials. But they wouldn't use it if it didn't work.

Like certain spectators at auto races who are there mainly to see the crashes, there are some who turn on the news just to see and hear about the latest social or global wreck. Sadly, when the disparaging news is interrupted by a report about something good, such as an organization helping the poor or feeding the hungry, they head to the fridge to get a snack that will sustain them until the next bad news alert.

My preference is to take a break from the breaking news, and I've found that going outdoors is a great way to do it. One spring day I decided to turn the TV off and go chase gobblers at a nearby farm. During the hunt I walked by an old cemetery on the backside of the property. Most of the people in the plot were from two families with extended history in the county. Feeling wearied by all the political arguing that filled the airways, I whispered to the deceased, "At least you don't have to hear the hateful bickering, deceit, and ugliness that just won't stop!"

Before I could finish my sentence, I thought about some loved ones who had recently died, including my father as well as a good friend. I also thought of Annie's parents, who had been gone for a few years, and my grandparents, who left us decades ago. When their faces passed through my mind, I added, "And you too! Right now none of the stuff on the news is of any concern to you. Enjoy your rest!"

What a marvelous thing my departed family and friends have experienced by being "taken away from evil." They have entered into peace and now "rest in their beds." I certainly don't have a death wish, but I must say that the idea of sharing in their advantage of never hearing the words BREAKING NEWS again certainly helps lessen the dread of dying.

There is, of course, one good reason people will experience the eternal blessing of peace and rest that comes from being "taken away from evil." It's because of God's grace offered only through Christ that redeems us and helps us walk uprightly before Him until our journey through time is finished. The joy of being present in heaven with our holy God and eternally separated from evil is a benefit I long to enjoy. May it be so for me and for you as well.

Thank You, God, for the day that the terrible BREAKING NEWS was replaced with the GOOD NEWS of redemption through Christ. Through Him alone, I have the hope of someday being taken away from evil and being truly at rest. Help me to walk uprightly in Your grace until that day. In the name of Christ I pray. Amen.

Strutters

*You, Lord, will keep the needy safe
and will protect us forever from the wicked,
who freely strut about
when what is vile is honored by the human race.*

Psalm 12:7-8 niv

Being a married man and an avid turkey hunter means that my non-hunting wife "gets to" listen to the post-hunt stories I seem compelled to tell. As a result, she has become familiar with some terms that relate to chasing the birds. One of them came up in a conversation on a spring morning over coffee in our sunroom.

"Honey," Annie started, "did you know the word 'strut' is in the Bible?"

"You're kidding!" I honestly didn't know.

Annie put her coffee cup down as she reached for her Bible and said, "No, really. It's in Psalm 12:7-8, and it doesn't put strutting in a good light. Let me read it to you. 'You, Lord, will keep the needy safe and will protect us forever from the wicked, who freely strut about when what is vile is honored by the human race.'"

She emphasized the word "strut" and then looked at me. I was smiling as I responded.

"How cool that you found a 'turkey word' in the Scriptures—and you thought of me. I'm honored!"

She smiled back then picked up her cell phone and did a quick web search of the meaning of "strut." A few seconds later, she said, "It says here that 'strut' means a stiff, apparently arrogant, conceited gait." She put her phone down and added, "I have to admit, whenever I've been with you in the car and you point out a strutting gobbler in a field, it sure looks like pride has him all puffed up. But according to you it's not pride; it's the presence of a receptive hen. In other words, they're *motivated* to strut!"

I raised my eyebrows and responded, "Oh, yes ma'am, they're definitely motivated! Nothing sinful about it though. Those boys are just doing what comes natural."

My clever wife grinned as she said, "I'm glad God didn't make human males to do such a thing. That would be a disturbing sight to see!"

I totally agreed. She continued.

"So if it takes motivation to strut, then the wicked mentioned in the verses certainly had it, but what drove them to do it was not only sinful, it was dreadful. The verse says that they strutted about because evil was not just present; it was promoted by men."

Neither of us said anything for a few seconds. Each of us seemed to know what the other was thinking. Before I could say it aloud, Annie spoke up.

"All we have to do to see some strutters like those mentioned in Psalm 12 is to turn on the evening news. When I see people in our nation arrogantly shouting with joy over the acceptance of debauchery or defiantly celebrating the death of the innocent while calling on others to join their evil cause, then what I'm seeing is the wicked strutting in the streets. They sure do give turkeys a bad name!"

I love that woman—and ever since that morning with Annie over coffee, I've not seen a strutting gobbler the same way again.

Dear God, thank You for Your willingness to protect us from the wicked who haughtily promote evil. My prayer is that You will destroy their works by bringing them to the knowledge of Your saving grace. Nothing and no one else could change them like You can. May it be so to Your glory alone. In Christ's name, amen.

· 46 ·

The Good Enemy

The LORD *your God is the one who goes with you, to*
fight for you against your enemies, to save you.

DEUTERONOMY 20:4

One of the greatest things about sitting quietly in the great outdoors is having the time and opportunity to watch things happen in nature, live and in color. It's a view that even the biggest television or theater screen can't provide. Even better, those things sometimes bring to life one of the many important truths found in the written Word of God. Here's a favorite example.

One day during spring turkey season, around midmorning, I took a seat against the wide trunk of an oak tree at the edge of a field on our neighbor's farm. After about fifteen minutes of waiting to see if some hens might lead some gobblers into the open area, I heard a high-pitched screech above me. I looked up and saw an unusual sight.

A sizable crow was flying erratically, trying to fend off an attack by two irate mockingbirds that were alternately dive-bombing him. I assumed the crow had tried to invade their nest and grab some eggs or maybe little hatchlings, and I figured the sky-pecking he was getting was well deserved. I rooted for the pair of defenders as they screamed something at the crow in bird language that probably should not be interpreted.

The two-bird mobbing I watched was a real-time illustration of the ancient saying, "The enemy of my enemy is my friend." No doubt each bird was grateful for the other's help as they fought their nest-saving war against the airborne thief. As the crow flew into the distance and the duo returned wing to wing to the woods behind me, I imagined one saying triumphantly to the other, "Give me a high feather...put it here!"

The connection this aerial battle scene has to our lives as humans is obvious. When we're facing an enemy, it's wonderful to find someone who dislikes our foe as much as we do.

I experienced this once when I nearly stepped on a poisonous snake on a friend's back steps at his rural home. He hurriedly got his shotgun and eliminated the threat for me. He was truly being the enemy of my enemy.

That creepy, slithering, poisonous adversary is not the only foe I have. I have another nemesis who is far more formidable—the devil himself. According to John 10:10, his mission is to steal, kill, and destroy. Like you, I am on his hit list. But the good news is, we can rejoice that we have a friend in Jesus who is the enemy of our enemy.

As our Savior, Jesus stepped in and defeated the devil once and for all through His willing death on the cross, His burial, and His resurrection. That means that whenever or however our enemy tries to destroy us, our sure defense is in the promise given in 1 Corinthians 15:57: "Thanks be to God, who gives us the victory through our Lord Jesus Christ."

Maybe the next time you see a big black crow being tormented in flight by a couple of smaller birds (or a buddy swoops in and blasts a venomous snake for you—yikes!), you'll remember the blessing of having Christ as the enemy of your enemy. Oh, what a friend we have in Jesus!

Jesus, what a blessing it is to know that You are the enemy of my enemy the devil. That truth makes my friendship with You even more eternally vital and valuable. I want to stay close to You. It's the only sure place of safety for me. Blessed be Your powerful name. Amen.

47

Turkey Toddlers

*Jerusalem, Jerusalem, you who kill the prophets and
stone those sent to you, how often I have longed to
gather your children together, as a hen gathers her
chicks under her wings, and you were not willing.*

LUKE 13:34 NIV

In my opinion there's hardly anything cuter in the animal kingdom than a wild turkey poult. In our neck of the woods, the twenty-eight-day incubation period ends sometime in mid to late May, so the prime time to catch a glimpse of a freshly hatched turkey is in June and July.

Seeing a turkey poult's little legs work fast and hard to keep up with its mama and siblings as they cross a low-cut field or a country road makes me stop whatever I'm doing and enjoy the show. I should have a warning sign on the rear bumper of my truck that says, "I brake for turkey toddlers!"

On the rare occasions that I've seen a hen and her poults, the adorable sight has moved me to say, "Ahh, lookie there!" It's as though I can't stop the words from coming. The scene can produce such a spontaneous reaction, it's no wonder Jesus would use such tender imagery as He lamented over Jerusalem. The city was filled with those who rejected him as their Messiah, so He groaned as He said, "How often I have longed to gather your children together, as a hen gathers her chicks under her wings, and you were not willing."

Jesus chose an effective metaphor to illustrate the emotion He felt. He surely knew that the mental picture of a hen with her chicks would tenderize the hearts of every person in earshot. It certainly melts mine today, and there's no reason to think it didn't do the same back then.

There's no other way to interpret what Jesus said than as an expression of His intense love for the people He had visited. His mission was to save them from both earthly and eternal destruction. But they didn't know it, and instead of accepting Him, they would soon kill Him. That, too, likely caused Him to weep.

The question is, does the compassion Jesus felt for the lost ones who had gathered for the Passover in Jerusalem extend to those who are spiritually lost now? According to 2 Peter 3:9, the answer is a comforting yes. The verse says, "The Lord is not slow about His promise, as some count slowness, but is patient toward you, not wishing for any to perish but for all to come to repentance."

Perhaps the next time your soul is moved by the sight of a mother turkey and her lovable little poults scampering around her, you'll let it remind you of how much Jesus wants you to believe that He is the Messiah, the Blessed One who came to redeem all sinners. He longs for us to accept Him and to let Him gather us in so that He can give us the blessing of protection under His mighty wings.

Father, thank You for sending Your holy Son to the earth so that I can believe in Him and be restored to a relationship with You. How kind You are to show Your great love for me through such a tender picture as a hen and her chicks. Blessed be Your name. Amen.

48

Bike Bait

*Every man is tempted, when he is drawn away of his
own lust, and enticed. Then when lust hath conceived,
it bringeth forth sin: and sin, when it is finished,
bringeth forth death. Do not err, my beloved brethren.*
JAMES 1:14-16 KJV

The half dozen plump smallmouth bass on my stringer were plenty for the fryer, so I decided to pack up and head home. I noticed that I had one red wiggler left in the plastic tub and started to toss it into the lake as a free snack for the fish. Instead, I decided not to waste my bait.

With a red-and-white round bobber just six inches above the freshly baited hook, I gently tossed the combination only a few feet from the shore. The water was clear, so I could see the dangling worm below the surface. Within a matter of seconds, I saw a flash of greenish silver dart beneath the bobber. In the next moment, it disappeared and the line went tight.

I really didn't have to set the hook because the fast-fleeing, bait-thieving fish did it for me when he ran out of slack in the line. Less than two minutes after dropping the worm in the well-populated lake, I was adding a soon-to-be-tasty, hand-size bluegill to the stringer that was already heavy with bass.

What a total shock it must have been for the darting fish when he was instantly stopped by the violent sideways jerk on his jaw. Imagining the sudden surprise reminds me of a human version of the same scenario I saw on the internet. It was in a video clip of a thief being caught.

The video creators leaned an expensive bicycle against a tree in a city park and left it unsecured and unguarded. At least that was the intended impression. What was not visible to passersby was the thin, strong, and well-concealed twenty-yard tether that ran from the bike's lower frame to a nearby concrete post.

The amateur videographers hid and waited for an unscrupulous bait taker to show up. Before long a bait thief walked by, saw the bike was unguarded, looked around to see if anyone was watching, jumped on, and started quickly peddling away.

Though it was sad to watch the crime unfold, it was hard not to laugh when the criminal sped away—until the bike abruptly stopped at the end of the tether. The surprised rider flew head-long over the handlebars, and his facial expression showed complete shock as he crashed into the ground. Immediately after impact he jumped up and, with a deserved hobble, took off running.

Both the worm-thieving fish and the bike robber learned a hard lesson that can benefit us all. We all have some desires that, when fulfilled, have pleasurable beginnings but terrible endings. The difference between the fish and the fellow was that the bluegill didn't try to swim away with my night crawler because of sinful intent. He was just doing what hungry fish do, and his frying-pan consequence didn't have guilt and shame connected to it.

The guy who took the shiny, two-wheeled bait, however, knew he was doing wrong, which was evidenced by his visual check of the area to see if anyone was watching just before he mounted up and rode away. Unwilling to say no to his bike-lust, he gave in to the temptation, enjoyed it for twenty yards, and then suffered a painful downfall. It was obvious that he felt at least some level of guilt for his action because of the way he quickly limped away from the scene of the crime. Unfortunately, his shame and embarrassment were not kept private—the video he starred in went viral worldwide.

Sin often feels great at first. The excited expression on the face of the bike thief during his short getaway ride demonstrates that. But when sin runs its course, it truly does bring forth death. The death is sometimes physical, but in most cases it's spiritual. It's a demise I certainly want to avoid, and I suspect you do too. We can do so by following the advice of James, who said, "Do not err, my beloved brethren." Smart choice!

Almighty and all-seeing God, I never want to forget that Your eyes are on those who follow You. I desperately want to please You by not fulfilling desires that lead to spiritual death. Thank You for forgiving me in those times I've failed and allowed myself to be trapped in sin. I know I need the strength of Your grace to help me not err, and I ask for it now in Your loving name. Amen.

The Challenge Meter

Let endurance have its perfect result, so that you
may be perfect and complete, lacking in nothing.
JAMES 1:4

If turkey hunters could purchase a "challenge meter" to gauge the effort it takes to outsmart a mature gobbler, they'd think it was defective straight out of the box, and here's why. The wild turkey has extremely keen eyes and an intensely cautious nature, so the needle would already be leaning three-fourths to the right, hovering over the yellow caution area that warns, "Leave your ego at home."

From that point the chase just gets tougher. As the hunting pressure increases due to a constant parade of humans entering the bird's territory and overusing their artificial calling devices, the males get even more suspicious—and quiet. Consequently, when the big guys stop gobbling for the girls, the needle moves further right to the "You might wanna try fishing" warning.

When late season arrives and turkey hunting becomes a desperate game of "run and gun," the challenge meter needle shoots into the red range, where there's a picture of a strutting tom laughing wildly and mischievously pointing a wing at a dejected hunter.

Knowing that the last week of the season in Tennessee meant we would be in that red range, my friend and I went anyway for one last attempt to put turkey breast on our dinner table. It wasn't long before we found ourselves in a midmorning battle of wits with a sizable tom. We tried every trick in our collection of calls to entice him to leave the pair of females he was with, but he was in no way impressed with any of our hen impersonations. We finally resolved ourselves to the fact that ambushing him by getting out in front of him was our only hope, and to do so required hurrying around a huge patch of woods that would conceal our movement and noise.

The weight of our 12-gauge shotguns, the gear we were toting in the pockets of our turkey vests, and the head-to-toe camo we wore on this warm May morning resulted in a sweat-drenched arrival at the spot where we wanted to set up and wait for the gobbler. We could only hope it would be worth the strain.

About ten minutes after we sat down under the dark shade of a couple of leafy scrub trees at the edge of the field, my friend delivered a load of buckshot that sent gobbler feathers flying and two surprised hens running for the hills. Our efforts resulted in some fresh and tasty wild turkey meat to enjoy later—as well as a vigorous high five, a few loud whoops and hollers, and some knee-slapping happiness for the two of us.

Why such an energetic on-site celebration? Ultimately it was the far right leaning of the needle on our "challenge meter" telling us the hunt wouldn't be easy. We were forced to persevere if we expected to enjoy the benefits of success. Endurance had, as James 1:4 calls it, "its perfect result." For us turkey hunters, that was the really good feeling that came with staying with the pursuit until the shot was taken. Plus, successfully outwitting the gobbler yielded some added knowledge to use for future pursuits.

These benefits provide an immensely satisfying feeling for any hunter, but they don't begin to compare to the depth of joy that a follower of Christ can know when he or she lets "endurance have its perfect result." Whether it's a concern about health, a relational or financial struggle, or any other strength-consuming issue, God can provide the stamina to help His followers press on. And for those who do, James 1:4 promises the incredibly valuable outcome of being made "perfect [mature] and complete, lacking in nothing." That's a huge trophy in any hunter's record book!

Thank You, Lord, for the gift of Your strength that You offer to those who follow You. I trust that You are aware of where the needle is on my heart's challenge meter and that You know the help I need to be victorious in this life. I want to be spiritually mature, and I need the wisdom that results from closely following You. May it be so to Your glory. In Christ's name I pray. Amen.

$\cdot$ 50 $\cdot$

Same Spirit

*If the Spirit of Him who raised Jesus from the
dead dwells in you, He who raised Christ Jesus
from the dead will also give life to your mortal
bodies through His Spirit who dwells in you.*

ROMANS 8:11

The phone call from Paul Meeks was a welcome surprise. He's
a friend and fellow hunter as well as an outdoor industry icon
from Louisiana who created and manufactured my all-time favorite climbing tree stand, the Grand Slam. His purpose for connect-
ing was to invite me to join him in his company's booth during a
huge hunting expo in Nashville.

As we sat behind his display tables, we enjoyed catching up on
what was happening with our families. I didn't mind frequently
pausing our chat so he could answer questions from the event
attendees who stopped to check out his products. It's why he was
there, and I was delighted to see all the interested outdoor-loving
men and women who stopped by.

As Paul was talking to a couple of guys, I noticed quite a buzz of
activity across the aisle and a couple of booths down. The action was

at the sizable corner booth of a popular camouflage clothing company. People were rushing to get in a line that was quickly forming
at a table. I didn't know why until I saw two men sit down at the
booth's celebrity meet-and-greet area.

I immediately recognized the gentlemen as they started signing
autographs and posing for pictures with their fans. In the hunting
world, these two guys are considered rock stars. It would be diffi-
cult to number how many times I'd seen them on TV and in videos. They traveled the world, filming hunts for deer, turkey, elk, bear,
sheep, goats, ducks, geese—you name it.

As huge as they were in the hunting community, I could see that
their stardom had not soured their attitude toward people. I was
impressed by how friendly and accommodating they were to each
person they met. Paul and I enjoyed watching the hubbub and how
big the eyes were of those who stood next to their well-known hunting heroes.

The big buzz in the neighboring booth demonstrated that the
hunting world does indeed have its celebrities, and many of us
would probably give just about anything to be one of them. Unfortunately, that's not going to happen for me, but I actually have a lot
in common with the rock-star hunters. In my soul is the very same
"spirit of the wild" and passion for the outdoors that they feel. The
only difference is that I don't have the endorsements and free gear
(and perhaps the expertise) they have.

In a similar and far more important way, however, I do have
celebrity status, and it comes with some amazing benefits. The following two verses from Romans and 1 Peter explain.

- "If the Spirit of Him who raised Jesus from the dead
  dwells in you, He who raised Christ Jesus from the dead
  will also give life to your mortal bodies through His
  Spirit who dwells in you" (Romans 8:11).

- "You are a chosen race, a royal priesthood, a holy nation, a people for God's own possession, so that you may proclaim the excellencies of Him who has called you out of darkness into His marvelous light" (1 Peter 2:9).

According to these verses, those of us who belong to Jesus have the very same power that gave life to His mortal body at His resurrection. What a marvelous thought! By embracing the truth about Christ, who now dwells in us, we are made to be a royal priesthood. This astonishing truth indeed gives us a celebrity status that cannot be matched by anyone or anything else in this world.

I'm hopeful that as you keep the truths of these passages in mind, you'll never see an outdoor celebrity the same way again. I certainly won't.

Father in heaven, thank You for pouring the Holy Spirit into me and giving me new and abundant life. It is indeed amazing to think that I have within me the same Spirit who brought Jesus out of the tomb. And thank You that because of my relationship with You through Your holy Son, I am seen in Your eyes as royalty. I bless You for being so generous to me. Amen.

51

In or *For*—It's a Choice

In everything give thanks; for this is
God's will for you in Christ Jesus.
1 THESSALONIANS 5:18

When I returned from an elk hunt in Colorado without an ounce of meat or an inch of antlers to show for all the effort and expense, my wife was surprised to discover that I was not depressed about it in the least. Instead, I was quite pleased with the outcome. When she asked me about my unexpected reaction, I read to her the email I sent to the gentleman who had arranged the hunt.

After I finished reading, she said, "It sounds to me like you've followed the advice in 1 Thessalonians 5:18. It doesn't say, '*For* everything give thanks.' It says, '*In* everything give thanks.' You've chosen to see the good in your time in Colorado in spite of coming home empty-handed. I appreciate it, and I'm sure both the landowner and the Lord do too."

Annie then said, "Maybe you should share the email with other hunters who might put a lot of effort into a trip that was disappointing. It might help them see what it looks like to give thanks *in* everything rather than *for* everything."

At her suggestion, here is the email.

. . . .

Cecil,

Steve Chapman here. I got home to Tennessee last night after hunting on your property in Colorado. I just wanted to say that even though I didn't fill my tag, I had one of the best hunts I've had in a long time. Here's why.

I've enjoyed guided hunts in high country before, but often the guide did all the hunting and calling, and I was basically the "trigger guy." Though I didn't get to be the one who actually found the animals, those high-country guided hunts were satisfying because of the incredible scenery, the horses, the base camp, and of course, the kills.

As you know, the area I just finished hunting is quite different from the higher elevations. Though there were no tall and majestic spruce, no high rocky cliffs and giant snowy peaks to observe up close, the property was beautiful in its own unique way. But the greater reason I so enjoyed the hunt is that I got do what I LOVE to do. I actually got to be the hunter. I got to go to a new property. I spent the first few days really getting to know it by walking around, studying the terrain, looking for signs of critter presence and movement, and developing a strategy.

The warm weather and relatively few hunters in the surrounding area that could have driven the elk down to lower elevation and moved them around for us were definitely disadvantages (which we fully understand could not have been predicted). Consequently, we didn't spot a single elk…until day four. That's when the process I so enjoy paid off. While taking my time to walk and glass, I spotted a bull on the far backside of the property a little after noon (I may have jumped him out of his bed) and got to engage in an unforgettable battle of wits with him. He looked to be a five-by-five and maybe bigger, but my binocs were shaking from excitement so much that it was tough to tell. I do know he was a legal bull.

I was exposed when I first saw him and dared not move as he looked my way. The shot would have been uphill beyond 350 yards, and the motion required to sit down to get a good rest for my rifle would have surely spooked him. I chose to just watch and wait to see which way he was headed so I could move ahead of him for a closer encounter. When he disappeared into the brush, I hightailed it to where I thought he'd reappear. It required a tough, hurried, long climb, but I was sure I got there in good time.

After an hour of wide-eyed waiting with my thumb on the safety, he didn't show. It took a little while to descend into the draw and climb up to a vantage point on the opposite side so I could watch the area where I had last seen him. I took a seat and waited, thinking maybe he had bedded down at that spot. Around five thirty in the evening, I was very gratified to see the distinct form of his huge body moving again in the brush. What a thrill it was not just to see him once more but to know I had guessed right. That in itself was a great moment.

At that point he was probably 800 yards away and feeding. I thought sure he would drop down into the draw to water before sunset after he fed. I watched his head movement, and each time he looked down at the grass, I slowly repositioned. I ended up about a hundred yards from where I expected him to drink. However, he didn't do what I thought he would, at least not in legal daylight. I headed out in the dark empty-handed, but my heart was full of happiness because of the contest I had just enjoyed. Plus, I could hardly wait till the next morning!

I went back to that area again on day five but didn't see him or another elk. But the anticipation of it was huge, and that too was very satisfying. Having learned that elk were in the area as a result of doing what it took to find the sign made the anticipation doubly strong.

I should add that as it turned out, on the last morning of the hunt I discovered that had I been able to take the shot where I first saw the bull, he would have been about seventy-five yards beyond the property fence. If I had connected, perhaps there would have been some forgiveness and mercy for that mistake because the fence was not clearly visible, but it would have put a big "if" on the experience for me—and it may have been a problem for you. I wouldn't have wanted that outcome. I'd much rather have downed the bull in the area of the watering hole, which would have left no question about the kill.

Bottom line…for me it was a most enjoyable experience because I actually spent four and a half days doing nothing but hunting hard. It was a mind-clearing, soul-stirring, spirit-inspiring experience. The climbs and descents were tough and tested my aging legs and heart, but I absolutely loved it. It would have been good to have added the backbreaking work of packing out some tasty elk meat, but I had a GREAT time and didn't have a mess to clean!

Sorry to bend your ear with a long email, but I just wanted to offer a detailed thanks for the memories…and blessings on your journey.

Steve Chapman

> *Father in heaven, You are the God of all that is good. I pray that my eyes will always be open to see the good in what may appear to lack goodness. I yield my attitude about this to You and ask You to shape it into one that is always pleasing in Your sight. For the sake of letting others see the light of Your hope in me, help me always to choose to give thanks in all things. Amen!*

52

God of My Father

To You, O God of my fathers, I give thanks and praise,
For You have given me wisdom and power;
Even now You have made known to me what we
requested of You,
For You have made known to us the king's matter.

DANIEL 2:23

O n the walls of my man cave are remembrances of a few of my hunts I like to tell about. I've mounted a gobbler fan and two of that tom's four beards. I'm not sure what happened to the other two beards when my friend pulled the trigger of his 12-gauge, so it's hard to prove that the monster bird sported almost thirty inches of beard, but it's true.

The fan and beard display is special because it represents a major sacrifice—though it was, I confess, unintentional. The short version of the story is, my buddy and I spotted the giant gobbler and decided it was going to wander across a big field toward us to one of two spots. I sent my friend to where I thought the bird would go, and I took the less likely setup, hoping with all my heart I would be wrong. As it turned out, I was right, and my buddy bagged the bird. He had it mounted and gave it to me for my wall of fame as his thanks for my inadvertent generosity.

Then there's a sizable eight-point whitetail rack mounted European style that I took in Michigan as a part of a TV show. At the time it was the biggest whitetail I had tagged, and the footage made a great episode.

Another wall is half covered by a nine-foot brown bear rug. Its home was in the Last Frontier State, and the story that goes with the hunt is in my book *My Dream Hunt in Alaska*.

In another part of our residence are two sets of heavy elk antlers, a vicious-looking javelina head, a fat red squirrel, and a beastly head mount of a South Dakota mule deer.

Along with the nicely preserved dead things hanging around, I have photo books that feature images taken on the days the tags were filled. I also have trays of videos in various formats, from analog to digital, that contain film from hunts that span more than twenty-five years. And our shelves are filled with souvenir copies of the many books I've written about my time in the great outdoors.

As grateful as I am for the many adventures I've had as a hunter, and as careful as I've been to display the evidence of my encounters with wild things, the truth is, they're not what I want most as my legacy. Instead, I want to be remembered for the same thing my late father is remembered for. I wrote this song lyric about him, and it explains what I mean.

God of My Father

I am his child
I watched him all of my life
One thing is certain
He was a lover of the Light
But I heard before I came along, he was lost out in the
   dark

Till someone led him to the cross, then he gave the
   Lord his heart

There were changes
All his friends could tell
They said he kept on drinking
He just chose a different well
They said he kept going out at night but drove past
   that neon sign
To the church where he left his guilt and all his shame
   behind

The God of my father saved him from his sins
The God of my father put a sweet love down in him
And it made him the kind of man that makes me want
   to follow
The God of my father

Now here I stand
Where his name is on a stone
I've come to give my thanks again
That I grew up in his home
And when it's my turn to rest here, this one thing I
   pray
That a child of mine could come along and think of
   me and say...

The God of my father saved him from his sins
The God of my father put a sweet love down in him
And it made him the kind of man that makes me want
   to follow
The God of my father[10]

If my children and my grandchildren can begin a prayer the way Daniel did when he said, "To You, O God of my fathers," it will be only because they recognize in me the God whom my earthly father also loved and served. If so, that's when I will know that I too have been successful in leaving a good and godly legacy. Beyond that, nothing else really matters.

O God of my father, blessed be Your great and mighty name for Your intervention in my life that allowed me the honor of knowing You and passing on the knowledge of You to my children. I know that no success is greater than leaving a legacy of Your love in the lives of those I call family. I pray for Your grace and strength to help me stay close to You for the rest of my days so that I will bring no reproach on Your good name. May it be so to Your glory alone. In Your Son's holy name I pray. Amen.

Notes

1. Steve Chapman, "Pray for the One You Got," © 2017 Times & Seasons Music/ BMI. Used by permission.

2. Steve Chapman, "Tell My Boy Hello for Me," © 2017 Times & Seasons Music. Used by permission.

3. Elwood McQuaid, *Not to the Strong* (Westville, NJ: Friends of Israel Gospel Ministry, 1991), 34. Used by permission.

4. Steve Chapman, "In Just a Little While," © 2017 Times & Seasons Music. Used by permission.

5. Steve Chapman and Dana Bacon, "Available," © 2017 Times & Seasons Music and Dana Bacon Music. Used by permission.

6. Steve Chapman, "Life Goes Around," © 2017 Times & Seasons Music. Used by permission.

7. Steve Chapman, "Real Good Life," © 2017 Times & Seasons Music. Used by permission.

8. Steve Chapman, "He Loves to Preach," © 2017 Times & Seasons Music. Used by permission.

9. Steve Chapman, "Moments of Heaven," © 2017 Times & Seasons Music. Used by permission.

10. Steve Chapman, "God of My Father," © 2017 Times & Seasons Music. Used by permission.

More Great Harvest House Hunting Books by Steve Chapman

365 Things Every Hunter Should Know

Another Look at Life from a Deer Stand

Great Hunting Stories

The Hunter's Cookbook

The Hunter's Devotional

A Look at Life from a Deer Stand

A Look at Life from a Deer Stand Devotional

A Look at Life from a Deer Stand Gift Edition

A Look at Life from a Deer Stand Study Guide

A Look at Life from the Riverbank

My Dream Hunt in Alaska

One-Minute Prayers® for Hunters

Stories from the Deer Stand

The Tales Hunters Tell

Tell Me a Huntin' Story

With Dad on a Deer Stand

With God on a Deer Hunt

STEVE'S BOOKS ABOUT FAMILY

10 Ways to Prepare Your Son for Life

52 Prayers for My Grandchild

A Dad's Guide to Praying for His Kids

The Good Husband's Guide to Balancing Hobbies and Marriage

Hot Topics for Couples

I Love You and I Like You

What Husbands and Wives Aren't Telling Each Other

STEVE'S BOOKS OF HUMOR

Down Home Wit and Wisdom

Wasn't It Smart of God to...

To learn more about Harvest House books and
to read sample chapters, visit our website:

www.harvesthousepublishers.com

HARVEST HOUSE PUBLISHERS
EUGENE, OREGON